Ottoman Women

Myth and Reality

Ottoman Women

Myth and Reality

ASLI SANCAR

THE Light

In loving memory of my mother, Myrtle Elizabeth Wood,
and my beloved son, Şahin Rıfat Sancar.

Published by The Light, Inc.

26 Worlds Fair Dr. Unit C

Somerset, New Jersey, 08873, USA

www.thelightpublishing.com

www.OttomanWomen.com

Art Director Engin Çiftçi

Graphic Design İhsan Demirhan, İbrahim Akdağ

Library of Congress Cataloging-in-Publication Data

Sancar, Asli.

Ottoman women : myth and reality / Asli Sancar.

   p. cm.

Includes bibliographical references and index.

ISBN 978-1-59784-115-3

1. Women--Turkey--History. 2. Women--Turkey--Social conditions. I. Title.

HQ1726.7.S26 2007

305.48>894350903--dc22

2007040138

Printed by

Çağlayan A.Ş., Izmir - Turkey

PAGE 2: Textile detail. Topkapı Palace Museum.

Contents

Introduction

Ottoman women have long been a subject of strong controversy. While the Orientalist view has portrayed them as exotic, indolent and depraved, some of their admirers have put them on a pedestal and practically relegated them to the realm of angels. Initially Ottoman women were a subject of disinterested curiosity for me. Having lived in Turkey for close to two decades, I had heard frequent references to the Ottomans and Ottoman society, usually very polarized ones that painted them either black or white. Some referred to the Ottomans as noble, enlightened exemplars of mankind, while others, particularly the official view, portrayed them as the personification of backwardness and reactionaryism. Ottoman women were described as capable and dignified ladies by some and as submissive and suppressed women entrapped in the harem by others.

When I began reading European travelers' accounts regarding Ottoman society, I found the same divergent views. The Orientalist view again depicted the Ottomans as barbaric despots, at worst, and as naive infidels, at best. It was claimed that Muslim women were denied to have souls and that they were merely the chattels of their husbands. On the other hand, these views were later openly disclaimed by such female travelers as Lady Montague, Julia Pardoe, and Lucy Garnett who actually lived in Ottoman lands for significant periods of time. At the other end of the spectrum, they argued that Ottoman women were perhaps the freest in the universe and that the treatment of Turkish women should be an example to all nations.

◀ Osman Hamdi, *Girl Picking Lilacs*

The disparity between these two views became resolved only in the light of court records involving Ottoman women. Western scholars have led the way in the investigation of the legal rights of Ottoman women and the effectiveness of their use of the courts to protect those rights. Evidence so far overwhelmingly shows that Ottoman women, far from being suppressed and helpless members of society, were legally free agents who could and did frequently use the courts to defend their rights, even against their husbands and other male relatives, if need be. There are examples of women coming to Istanbul from as far away as Egypt to petition the Sultan for redress of injustices when they could not get satisfactory legal results locally.

In view of the image of Ottoman women that is reflected in court records, I could no longer remain "disinterested" regarding them. I found in the Ottoman woman a female model that transcends time and place. Physically and in demeanor she was extremely feminine, graceful and refined. However, in spirit she was a fighter, a staunch and courageous defender of her God-given rights. Both her masculine and feminine natures were highly developed and in balance, which enabled her to act as a powerful pillar in the family and play an extremely important, if not visible, role in the social structure. In short, she was neither the demon nor the angel she had been portrayed to be, but rather a highly developed human being who lived her feminine nature to the fullest and who was appreciated and respected as a woman.

Today, at a time when women worldwide are casting aside an image that has constrained them for centuries and are searching for a new and better identity, the Ottoman woman offers a powerful model of how to be. She had a deep and abiding connection with her Creator, which compelled her to manifest the All-Merciful's Compassion and Love, at times, and the Almighty's Majesty and Power at other times. Of course, women's social parameters have changed today; however, the principles that molded the Ottoman woman's identity are just as relevant to the twenty-first century as they were to former times.

Author's Note: The Ottoman Empire was a vast state that at its height spread to three continents – Africa, Europe and Asia. The Ottoman dynasty also ruled for an extraordinarily long period of six centuries (the end of the 13th to the beginning of the 20th). Since the term "Ottoman women" can be applied to a broad range of ethnicities, races and religions, it is difficult to claim that there is one homogeneous type. The women described in this book are mainly Muslim women concentrated in the heartland of the Ottoman Empire. Since there are very few visual representations of Ottoman women from the early and classical periods of the Empire, I have tried to capture the spirit of these Ottoman women—the beauty and refinement of their lives—by means of the paintings, gravures and photographs used.

Zonaro, *Amusement at Göksu* (after 1910)

I

Ottoman Women through Western Eyes

The Turkish wife has been called a slave and a chattel. She is neither. Indeed, her legal status is preferable to that of the majority of wives in Europe, and until enactments of a comparatively recent date, the English was far more of a chattel than the Turkish wife, who has always had absolute control of her property. The law allows to her the free use and disposal of anything she may possess at the time of her marriage, or that she may inherit afterwards. She may distribute it during her life or she may bequeath it to whom she chooses. In the eyes of the law she is a free agent. She may act independently of her husband, may sue in the courts or may be proceeded against, without regard to him. In these respects she enjoys greater freedom than her Christian sisters.[1]

Z. Duckett Ferriman, 1911

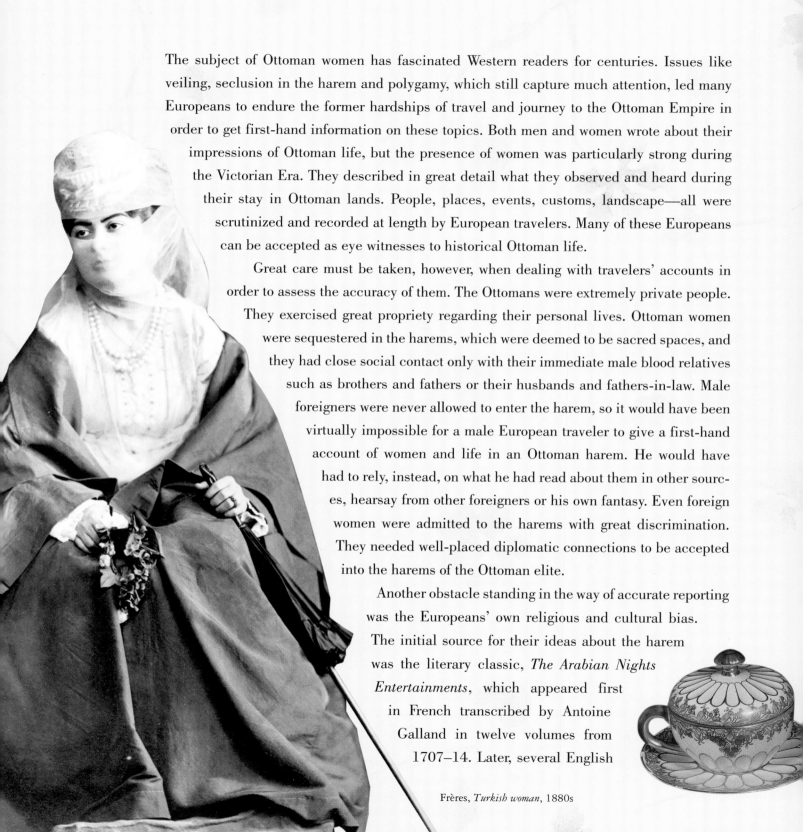

The subject of Ottoman women has fascinated Western readers for centuries. Issues like veiling, seclusion in the harem and polygamy, which still capture much attention, led many Europeans to endure the former hardships of travel and journey to the Ottoman Empire in order to get first-hand information on these topics. Both men and women wrote about their impressions of Ottoman life, but the presence of women was particularly strong during the Victorian Era. They described in great detail what they observed and heard during their stay in Ottoman lands. People, places, events, customs, landscape—all were scrutinized and recorded at length by European travelers. Many of these Europeans can be accepted as eye witnesses to historical Ottoman life.

Great care must be taken, however, when dealing with travelers' accounts in order to assess the accuracy of them. The Ottomans were extremely private people. They exercised great propriety regarding their personal lives. Ottoman women were sequestered in the harems, which were deemed to be sacred spaces, and they had close social contact only with their immediate male blood relatives such as brothers and fathers or their husbands and fathers-in-law. Male foreigners were never allowed to enter the harem, so it would have been virtually impossible for a male European traveler to give a first-hand account of women and life in an Ottoman harem. He would have had to rely, instead, on what he had read about them in other sources, hearsay from other foreigners or his own fantasy. Even foreign women were admitted to the harems with great discrimination. They needed well-placed diplomatic connections to be accepted into the harems of the Ottoman elite.

Another obstacle standing in the way of accurate reporting was the Europeans' own religious and cultural bias. The initial source for their ideas about the harem was the literary classic, *The Arabian Nights Entertainments*, which appeared first in French transcribed by Antoine Galland in twelve volumes from 1707–14. Later, several English

Frères, *Turkish woman*, 1880s

translations were made by British scholars, the most famous of which is Orientalist Sir Richard Burton's seventeen volumes published during 1882–86. The stereotypes of promiscuous and evil females drawn in *The Arabian Nights* greatly affected the reading public. This work and the many other translations of oriental tales and pseudo-tales that followed became the basis of the traditional Orientalist erotic image of the harem and the women in it.

Interestingly, the original source of *The Arabian Nights* is unknown. Galland suggested that the tales had come to Arabia from India via Persia. It is not known whether the work is the product of one author or whether it was a compilation of numerous authors. Moreover, the text was first published in Arabic approximately a century after the French version. Although the origin of *The Arabian Nights* is obscure, the impact it had on Western readers was immense. Together with editions of other oriental tales that quickly followed its publication (i.e., Turkish, Persian, Chinese tales, etc.), it prepared the foundation of the harem myth, which portrays oriental women as erotic and depraved creatures and the harem as the space in which this eroticism was played out. These stereotypes were repeated endlessly in European travelers' accounts and they still exist today, fed by sensationalist literary works that include recent semi-historical novels on the subjects of Ottoman women and the harem. The myth of the harem has been so successful that even most popular Turkish works on this subject repeat the same stereotypes.

Some European travelers, women in particular, beginning with Lady Montague who visited the Ottoman Empire from 1716–18 with her husband, the British ambassador to the Ottoman capital, were critical of those who based their writing on hearsay and fantasy instead of giving accurate reports to their readers. While describing Turkish houses in a letter to a Mrs. Thistlethwayte, she wrote, *"You will perhaps be surprised at an account so different from what you have been entertained with by the common voyage writers, who are very fond of speaking*

Lady Montague

11

of what they do not know. It must be under a very particular character, or on some extraordinary occasion, that a Christian is admitted into the house of a man of quality, and their harems are always forbidden ground."[2]

While describing the good conditions of Circassian slaves in a letter to Lady Rich, Montague underscored the same theme, *"I am afraid you will doubt the truth of this account, which I own, is very different from our common notions in England; but it is no less truth for all that."*[3]

Adept at criticizing those travelers who gave inaccurate reports regarding Turkey and the Ottoman people, Lady Montague, on the other hand, did not hesitate to bend the truth when it served her purpose. This was the case in her description of Ottoman women in the public bath in Sophia. Painting a neo-classical picture of statuesque nymphs for her readers, Montague presented the women as naked because they fit into her commentary better that way as a statement against the unnaturalness of Catholic attitudes in Britain toward female sexuality. Today's reader would probably take her observation at face value, but eighteenth-century readers would not have expected her description to be fully accurate. According to the editor of her works, J. A. St. John, Esq., her contemporary readers did not expect a wit like Lady Montague to pay complete regard to justice and the truth.[4]

Lady Montague's liberty with the truth regarding the nakedness of Ottoman women bathers was pointed out more than a century later by another famous British female traveler, Miss Julia Pardoe, who went to the Ottoman Empire in 1835 and spent close to fifteen months in Istanbul.

PAGE 10: Covered cup, 1902, Dolmabahçe Palace Museum

PAGE 11: Coffee table. 18th century

Mlle. Helene Glavany in Turkish Costume, 18th century ▶

Ewer and basin. Gold-plated copper, 18th century ▼

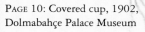

In reference to the bathing scene she wrote, *"I should be unjust did I not declare that I witnessed none of that unnecessary and wanton exposure described by Lady M. W. Montague. Either the fair Ambassadress was present at a peculiar ceremony, or the Turkish ladies have become more delicate and fastidious in their ideas of propriety."*[5]

Julia Pardoe, a poetess, historian and novelist, went to great lengths to describe Ottoman life accurately and to penetrate the surface of society to understand it on a deeper level. She was also critical of travelers who, generally unable to obtain first-hand interviews with the Ottoman elite, based their reports on erroneous and inadequate information from third parties. On this subject she wrote, *"There is perhaps no other country under heaven where it is more difficult for a European to obtain a full and perfect insight into the national character than in Turkey. The extreme application and length of time necessary to the acquirement of two leading languages, which bear scarcely any affinity to those of Europe, render the task one of utter hopelessness to the traveler, who consequently labors under the disadvantage of explaining his impressions and seeking for information through the medium of a third person, inferentially, and, it may almost be said, totally uninterested in both.... Thus the means of communication between the native and the stranger have an additional and almost insurmountable impediment in this respect, superadded to the natural and palpable obstacle presented by opposing and diffluent prejudices, customs, and opinions... I know not whether it may be from want of inclination, but it is certain that Europeans are at this moment resident in Turkey as ignorant of all that relates to her political economy, her system of government and her moral ethics as though they had never left their own country and who have nevertheless been resident there for fifteen or twenty years."*[6]

Pardoe was aware that it would be a difficult task to correct images and stereotypes of Ottoman life and society that had been engraved in the European consciousness through endless repetition over the years. The myths and fables regarding the East were much more enchanting than the truth. Pardoe concluded, *"The European mind has become so imbued with ideas of Oriental mysteriousness, mysticism, and magnificence, and it has been so long accustomed to pillow its faith on the marvels and metaphors of tourists, that it is to be doubted whether it will willingly cast off its old associations and suffer itself to be undeceived."*[7]

"The very term 'Oriental' implies to European ears the concentration of romance, and I was long in the East ere I could divest myself of the same feeling. It would have been easy for me to have continued the illusion, for Oriental habits lend themselves greatly to the deceit, when the looker-on is satisfied with glancing over the surface of things, but with a conscientious chronicler this does not suffice; and, consequently, I rather sought to be instructed than to be amused, and preferred the veracious to the entertaining...

"I would not remove one fold of the graceful drapery which veils the time-hallowed statue of Eastern power and beauty; but I cannot refrain from plucking away the trash and tinsel that ignorance and bad taste have hung about it, and which belong as little to the masterpiece they desecrate, as the votive offerings of bigotry and superstition form a part of one of Raphael's divine Madonnas because they are appended to her shrine."[8]

Another British female traveler, Lady Ramsey, defended the Turkish people against unfair claims made by Europeans as follows in her book, *Everyday Life in Turkey*, published in 1897: *"People have been accustomed lately to hear so much evil of the Turks—stories of their fanatical hatred towards their Christian fellow-countrymen, their cruelty and unspeakable wickedness—that one might well suppose them to be merely a sort of combination of ferocious wild beast and incarnate fiend. It is not under this aspect that I have known them and wish to speak of them. It is now seventeen years since I first went with my husband to Turkey. I have lived in the country, and have traveled in it, and have found the people always simple, peaceable, hospitable, and friendly—living amicably with their Christian neighbors."*[9]

Besides these women there are a number of other Europeans like Lucy Garnett, a British woman who spent seventeen years in Turkey during the reigns of Sultan Abdülmecid (1839–1861) and Sultan Abdülaziz (1861–1876), and M. de M. D'Ohsson, an Armenian who worked for many years in the Swedish Embassy during the eighteenth century, who had close contact with the Ottoman people and long experience in Ottoman society. Both Garnett and D'Ohsson spoke fluent Turkish and were generally unbiased in their approach. All of these Europeans can be considered as objective eye witnesses to Ottoman life, although, due to normal cultural bias, even their reports must be verified against other reliable accounts. Taken together, they present us with a colorful and authentic, if not fully complete, portrait of Ottoman women and Ottoman life.

Hilair, *Ladies of the harem taking a collation under a pavilion*, 1798 (?)

(Painter unknown), Young Woman, 18th century

Western Travelers' Descriptions of Ottoman Women

Physical Appearance

Z. Duckett Ferriman:

"Her beauty is of color rather than of line, though she can be very handsome. But it lies more than anything else in her intelligent expression. There are as many types of face as with us, but this characteristic is rarely lacking. In it, and in the simple dignity and grace of her manners, as well as in the charm with which she invests a melodious tongue, she has no rivals in the Near East, and few elsewhere. In the matter of physical type, she is of medium height, has small hands and feet, her hair is chestnut—she has a bad habit of dying it auburn—her eyes blue, gray or hazel, and more rarely brown. Her expression is usually placid. When she has a fiercer Roman style of beauty, it is nearly certain that she is of Circassian blood and slave origin. Her eyelashes are distinctly her own. The lower lash is as well developed as the upper—a very rare thing in the West—and sweeping a damask cheek, it gives her a distinction which the underlining of the eyes with 'surme' does not enhance, though she appears to think so."[10]

Miss Julia Pardoe:

"A short distance beyond the 'araba,' [cart] we came upon a beautiful young female, who had alighted from her carriage, and was kneeling upon a costly Persian prayer carpet, on whose eastern edge was placed a vase of wrought silver. Three slaves stood with folded arms, immediately behind her; and she was so completely absorbed in her devotions

that not even the apparition of a couple of European females, always objects of curiosity to a Turkish lady, caused her to lift her eyes. She was strikingly handsome, and her attitude was most graceful, as, with her small hands clasped together, she bowed her head to the earth in the deep, voiceless prayer which is the heart's offering, and requires not to shape itself into words. Had she been otherwise engaged, I could have lingered for an hour for the mere pleasure of looking upon one of the loveliest faces in the world."[11]

Lady W. M. Ramsey:

"I have been in one town where the population appeared to be about half Moslem and half Christian, and where, so far as I saw, none of the women were veiled and only a slight difference in the headdress marked the difference of race. This was at Koula, a place remarkable for its healthy climate and pure water, and a great summer resort for the inhabitants of the surrounding country. How pretty the women and girls were! With their fresh, rosy faces, their shining eyes and glossy hair, and their splendidly vigorous and handsome forms! I did not see a plain-looking one among them."[12]

Lady Montague:

"It must be owned that every kind of beauty is more common here than with us. It is surprising to see a young woman that is not handsome. They have naturally the most beautiful complexion in the world, and generally large black eyes. I can assure you with great truth that the court of England (though I believe it to be the fairest in Christiandom) does not contain so many beauties as are under our protection here. They generally shape their eyebrows; and both Greeks and Turks have the custom of putting round their eyes black tincture, that at a distance, or by candlelight, adds very much to the blackness of them. I fancy many of our ladies would be overjoyed to know this secret, but it is too visible by day. They dye their nails a rose color, but, I cannot enough accustom myself to the fashion to find any beauty in it."[13]

"But they were hardly seen near the fair Fatima, (for that was her name), so much her beauty effaced every thing I have seen, nay, all that has been called lovely either in England or Germany. I must own that I never saw any thing

Mirror, 16th century ▶

Osman Hamdi, *From Harem* (detail), 1880 ◄

so gloriously beautiful, nor can I recollect a face that would have been taken notice of near hers. She stood up to receive me, saluting me after their fashion, putting her hand to her heart with a sweetness full of majesty, that no court breeding could ever give. She ordered cushions to be given to me, and took care to place me in the corner, which is the place of honor. I confess, though the Greek lady had before given me a great opinion of her beauty, I was so struck with admiration that I could not for some time speak to her, being wholly taken up in gazing. That surprising harmony of features! That charming result of the whole! That exact proportion of body! That lovely bloom of complexion, unsullied by art! The unutterable enchantment of her smile! ...Add to all this, a behavior so full of grace and sweetness, such easy motions, with an air so majestic yet free from stiffness or affectation, that I am persuaded, could she be suddenly transported upon the most polite throne of Europe, nobody would think her other than born and bred to be a queen, though educated in a country we call barbarous. To say all in a word, our most celebrated English beauties would vanish near her."[14]

M. de M. D'Ohsson:

"The Turkish woman is not a slave of fashion that has lodged in the European woman's mind like a phantom. The same kind of headdress and the same style of clothing made from the same material are always used in Turkey. It shouldn't be a surprise that the people are tied this much to their customs and traditions, because the fashion tradesmen who constantly encourage indecision in other towns in the Empire by means of the variety of their creations cannot be found in Istanbul...

"At first sight Muslim women do not possess the elegance and attractiveness of European women. Yes, they cannot boast of this, but they can very well take pride in the simplicity and dignity of their clothing... Beautiful figures, dark and shiny eyes, and fresh ivory-like skin separate the women of this country from Europeans. Moreover, the beauty of their figures is not due to corsets, but they are always shapely and beautiful. Then, they do not resort to useless solutions to hide the signs of aging or disorderly passions either. Muslim women are unacquainted with rouge and lipstick. Only they like to paint half their nails with henna or 'kina' as it is called among the people. Also they use kohl on their eyebrows and, more often, on their eyelashes...

"Muslim women using artificial hairpieces are rarely to be found. Hairpieces and curls together with powder and cream, in a word items that are very important in the European's make-up, are strangers to the Turks. Hair is maintained in its natural shape. Either it falls down in long braids from the shoulders or it is wrapped around the muslin cloth that serves as headdress. Women with fifty, sixty or even eighty braids can be seen. The braids are usually adorned with flowers or every kind of precious stone.

"Almost all the women give great importance to embroidery not only in the items they use in their toilette, but in those things they use in their ordinary work as well. This is the case in everything from handkerchiefs, towels and napkins to undergarments and the belts to their trousers. In fact, men's are usually worked in silver or gold thread. Most women wear blouses artistically embroidered in silk."[15]

Refinement

Miss Julia Pardoe:

"Nothing can exceed the courtesy of the Turkish ladies to strangers. They appear delighted to converse with a European female who seems disposed to meet them half way; and they do so with a frankness and ease which at once destroy every feeling of 'gené' on the part of the stranger. In five minutes every thing they have is at your service; the fruit of which they are partaking, and the scented sherbet that they have prepared with their own hands. To make acquaintance with them, you require only to be cheerful, willing to indulge their harmless curiosity, and ready to return their civility in as far as you are able to do so. There is none of that withering indifference, or that supercilious scrutiny, which obtains so much in Europe, to

Marquis de Ferriol, *Woman Working Embroidery*, 1714

be dreaded from a Turkish gentlewoman; but there is, on the contrary, an earnest urbanity about her which is delightful, and which emanates from the intuitive politeness so universal among the natives; coupled with a simplicity of feeling, and a sincerity of good-nature, that lend a double charm to the courtesies of life. Nor is the eye less satisfied than the heart, in these moments of agreeable, although brief, communion; for the graceful bearing of an Oriental female greatly enhances the charm of her ready kindness; and her self-possession and dignity of manner, render her superior to the paltry affectation of assumed coldness; while they convince you that she would be as prompt to resent impertinence, as she had been ready to proffer courtesy."[16]

Z. Duckett Ferriman:

"Whatever may be said of the Turk, nobody can deny him his good manners. They are not the monopoly of a class. They are a national heritage, and are common to the peasant and the Pasha. In this respect the Turk is distinct from the other nationalities among which he lives and from the European as well."[17]

M. de M. D'Ohsson:

"Nature has given the Eastern woman both elegance and charm. Her manners are noble and elegant; her behavior is pleasing and her speech is simple, pure and refined. At least this is the consensus of Christian women who have the opportunity to visit Turkish harems frequently. There is no reason to believe that this is not the case. I, myself, have encountered Turkish women many times on specific occasions. Their simplicity of speech and ease of expression, the refinement of their thoughts, the elegance of their tone of voice and distinguished behavior always impressed me."[18]

Lucy Garnett:

"But not withstanding this absence of hereditary rank and class distinction—perhaps because of it—every Osmanli is both by nature and tradition an aristocrat, and the same dignity of bearing and courtesy of manner may be met with in the hovel of the peasant as in the 'konak' [mansion] of the Pasha."[19]

◀ Detail from a *sitil puşide*, a cover used while serving coffee in cups.

The Sultan's bath in the harem, Topkapı Palace

Cleanliness

Z. Duckett Ferriman:

"Cleanliness is a distinctive characteristic of the Turks. The abode may be humble, it may not even boast a carpet, but the grass matting will be swept, the tiles scrubbed, and pots and pans scoured with a thoroughness that recalls a Dutch household. You may eat, without apprehension, in a Turkish establishment of the simplest. It may be only a brazier and a few stools under a tree, but your two pennyworth of 'kebabs' will be served on a spotless platter with a snowy napkin... Turkish cleanliness is a national attribute."

Lucy Garnett:

"Personal cleanliness among Moslems certainly comes 'next to godliness,' being enjoined by the 'Sheriai,' [sharia] or Sacred Law; and to the regular and careful ablutions requisite for the maintenance of the condition of legal purity—in which certain religious acts may alone be performed—as also no doubt to their habitual temperance, are probably due the comparative freedom of the Turks from many of the ailments which afflict their Christian and Jewish neighbors. Several 'hammams,' as Turkish baths are termed, are to be found in every large town, and in the Capital they are numerous. A few—the mineral baths at Broussa [Bursa], for instance, and some of the older ones at Stamboul [Istanbul]—present fine examples of this species of architecture, and are much resorted to by all classes. The charges made to all are extremely moderate, and for the use of the poor there are numerous minor baths attached to mosques and other pious foundations at which they may perform their ablutions gratuitously."

M. de M. D'Ohsson:

"There is nothing comparable to the care both men and women give to the matter of washing and bathing almost every day. They do this for their own pleasure as much as to fulfill the religion's cleanliness requirements... I mentioned the cleanliness of the houses previously. Whether in the houses of prominent persons or ordinary people, wooden floors are all covered with carpets. The rest of the house is carefully scrubbed every week. Never can the slightest dirt, dust or mud be seen anywhere, because every man and woman, regardless of rank or position, takes off their shoes at the lower end of the stairs. In spite of the plainer floor coverings in official offices, the same attention is given to cleanliness. Besides these, coffee houses, shops, stores, workshops and public baths are just as clean."

◀ Copper tap, 18th century

▾ Clogs, 19th century

Miss Julia Pardoe:

"The most perfect cleanliness is the leading characteristic of Eastern houses—not a grain of dust, not a foot-mark, defaces

the surface of the Indian matting that covers the large halls, whence the several apartments branch off in every direction; the glass from which you drink is carefully guarded to avoid the possibility of contamination and, the instant you have eaten, a slave stands before you with water and a napkin to cleanse your hands. To the constant use of the bath I have already alluded and no soil is ever seen on the dress of a Turkish gentlewoman.”

Devoutness

Mary Adelaid Walker:

“*Some of her companions have also responded to the call of the 'muezzin,' others have let it pass unheeded; but the old fiction that Mussulmans [Muslims] deny that their women have souls is sufficiently refuted by the scrupulous care with which many amongst the inmates of a harem seek to ensure their future spiritual welfare by rigid observance of the appointed times of prayers, by obedience to the precept of frequent almsgiving, and by a strict observance of the very severe fast of Ramadan.*”[20]

Miss Julia Pardoe:

“*The Turkish women are intuitively pious; the exercises of religion are admirably suited to their style of existence. In the seclusion of the harem the hour of prayer is an epoch of unwearying interest to the whole of its inhabitants; and there is something touching and beautiful in the humility with which, when they have spread their prayer-carpets, they veil themselves with a scarf of white muslin, ere they intrude into the immediate presence of their Maker.*”[21]

“*The Osmanli is unostentatiously religious. He makes the great principles of his belief the rule of his conduct, and refers every thing to a higher power than that of man. I am aware that it is the fashion to decry the creed of the Turk, and to place it almost on a level of paganism: but surely this is an error unworthy of the nineteenth century, and of the liberality of Englishmen. The practice of a religion, which enforces the necessity of prayer and charity, which is tolerant of all opposing modes of worship, and which enjoins universal brotherhood, can scarcely be contemptible.*”[22]

"No occupation, whether of business or pleasure, is permitted to interfere with the religious duties of a Turkish female, however distinguished her rank; nor has locality or circumstance any influence in deterring her from their observance. It is a common occurrence to see the sister of the Sultan alight from her araba *[cart] at Kahaitchana [Kağıthane], or any other public place in which she may chance to find herself when her accustomed hour of prayer arrives; and, when her slaves have spread her prayer-carpet, kneel down within sight and sound of the crowds that throng the walk, as calmly and collectedly as though she were shut within one of the gilded chambers of her own Serai."*[23]

Hospitality and Generosity

M. de M. D'Ohsson:

"There are pious foundations in cities throughout the Empire, especially in Istanbul, which have been founded by the Sultan or other prosperous citizens to help the needy. The foundations' income is used continuously for this purpose. Not a day passes without Muslims giving charity or running to help those imprisoned for debt. Fathers, mothers, relatives and guardians from all classes of society are thus examples for the children, and the children have the trait of benevolence instilled in them at an early age. This divine virtue of benevolence, which makes people run to help their fellow man and forget their own interests, develops like this. This is an easy thing for the Turks to do and it raises them above other nations... Charity is an individual matter, but in spite of this, you will not find another people with such pure feelings, who are so charitable without expecting anything in return. It is not a desire for praise or ostentation that inspires the Turks; it is strictly their religious belief and humane feelings."[24]

Miss Julia Pardoe:

"Every one who has visited Turkey will perceive at once that I allude to their unbounded hospitality. The table of the greatest man in Constantinople is open to the poorest, whenever he chooses to avail himself of it. As he salutes the master of the house on entering, he is received with the simple word 'Bouroun'—You are welcome—and he takes his place without further ceremony. In the villages the same beautiful principle remains unaltered; and it signifies not how little an individual many have to give, he always gives it cheerfully, and as a matter

of course; without appearing conscious that he is exercising a virtue, practiced scantily and reservedly in more civilized countries."[25]

"*The never-failing hospitality of the East prompted the first question of the venerable hostess. She inquired if I had been satisfied with my reception; and assured me of the gratification she derived from seeing me in the Palace of her husband: she then thanked me for the careful toilette which I had made to visit her, and in the most courtly manner admired every thing that I wore.*"[26]

Modesty and Chastity

M. de M. D'Ohsson:

"*The careful protection of national tradition and customs by both the people and the police makes it impossible for women to lose the trait of modesty that is so natural for the fairer sex. A woman spends her time in the home. The windows facing the street are always covered with latticed shutters. Those who have gardens cannot go outside haphazardly. But all of this does not mean that a woman cannot leave her house. If a woman wants to go to the public bath, visit her parents, go shopping or just go out, she can. However, she cannot go out alone; other women, female slaves or eunuchs from the home accompany her. Elderly women can go out alone.*"[27]

Rogier, *Eating in the Harem*, 1848.

"Muslims behave so carefully regarding women's chastity that a woman whose behavior arouses even the slightest suspicion will begin to be looked down upon by every one. Even the smallest doubt is enough to make the husband and whole family humiliated. Moreover, the neighbors and others living in the vicinity will feel that their honor has been tarnished as well."[28]

"When all of this is taken into consideration, it can be clearly understood how impossible it is for there to be lover relationships among Muslims. Living with a woman who is not legally permitted or having an illicit sexual relationship with a girl is an unknown abnormality among Muslims. A man can never have a relationship with his wife's slave girl even if the woman has turned over all her property rights to her husband."[29]

Freedom

La Baronne Durand de Fontmagne:

"Turkish women are absolutely free. This truth can easily be seen. Those who say Turkish women are slaves deserve to be laughed at."[30]

Lady Montague:

"Upon the whole, I look upon the Turkish women as the only free people in the Empire; the very divan pays respect to them, and the grand signior himself, when a pasha is executed, never violates the privileges of the harem, (or women's apartment), which remains untouched and entire to the widow."[31]

Miss Julia Pardoe:

"If, as we are all prone to believe, freedom be happiness, then are the Turkish women the happiest, for they are certainly the freest individuals in the Empire. It is the fashion in Europe to pity the

Silver coffee pot, 19th century ▶

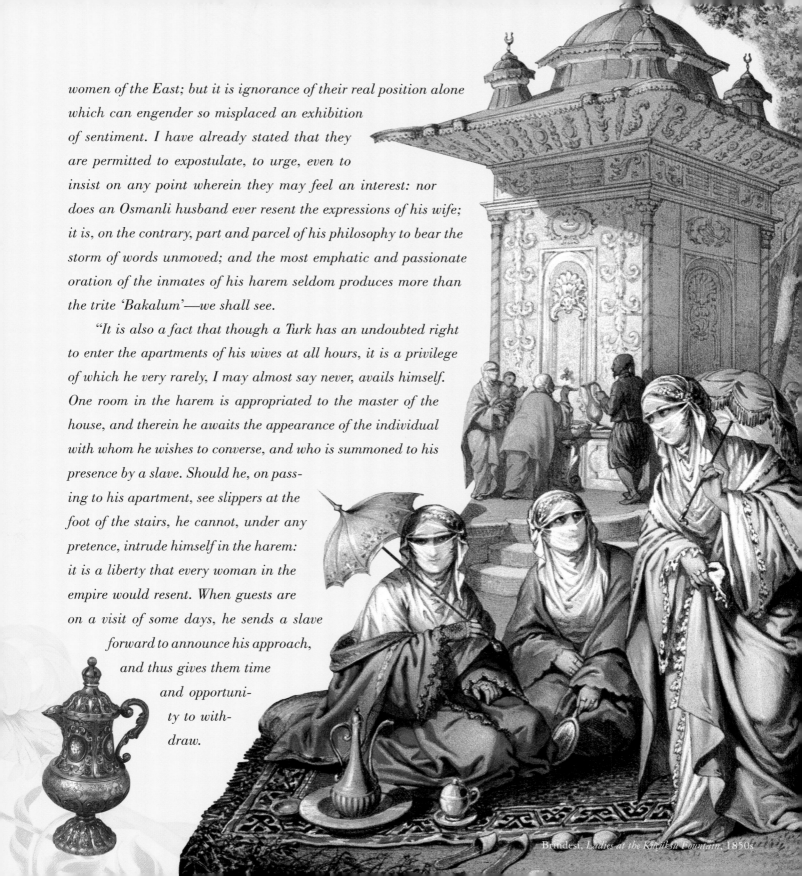

women of the East; but it is ignorance of their real position alone which can engender so misplaced an exhibition of sentiment. I have already stated that they are permitted to expostulate, to urge, even to insist on any point wherein they may feel an interest: nor does an Osmanli husband ever resent the expressions of his wife; it is, on the contrary, part and parcel of his philosophy to bear the storm of words unmoved; and the most emphatic and passionate oration of the inmates of his harem seldom produces more than the trite 'Bakalum'—we shall see.

"It is also a fact that though a Turk has an undoubted right to enter the apartments of his wives at all hours, it is a privilege of which he very rarely, I may almost say never, avails himself. One room in the harem is appropriated to the master of the house, and therein he awaits the appearance of the individual with whom he wishes to converse, and who is summoned to his presence by a slave. Should he, on pass-ing to his apartment, see slippers at the foot of the stairs, he cannot, under any pretence, intrude himself in the harem: it is a liberty that every woman in the empire would resent. When guests are on a visit of some days, he sends a slave forward to announce his approach, and thus gives them time and opportuni-ty to with-draw.

Brindesi, *Ladies at the Küçüksu Fountain*, 1850s

"A Turkish woman consults no pleasure save her own when she wishes to walk or drive, or even to pass a short time with a friend; she adjusts her 'yashmac' [veil] and 'feridje,' [dustcoat] summons her slave, who prepares her 'boksha,' or bundle, neatly arranged in a muslin handkerchief; and, on the entrance of the husband, his inquiries are answered by the intelligence that the Hanoum Effendi [mistress] is gone to spend a week at the harem of so and so. Should he be suspicious of the fact, he takes steps to ascertain that she is really there; but the idea of controlling her in the fancy, or of making it subject of reproach on her return, is perfectly out of the question."[32]

Love of Nature

Z. Duckett Ferriman:

"A distinctive trait in the character of the Turkish woman is her love for the open-air and the open country. In the mass it may be limited to the liking for shade, running water and flowers, but among the educated there is a feeling for the beautiful in nature, and, so far as the writer is aware, this is not shared by other Eastern women, certainly not in the same degree... A fine sunset will attract Turkish women, who gaze at it from every coign of vantage. This appreciation of the scenic side of nature is not confined to the educated. If the visitor to Constantinople cares to walk by the seawalls any fine evening, he will encounter group after group perched among the masses of masonry fallen from the ruined towers. They do not concern themselves with these. Antiquity does not appeal to them. They sit, for the most part silent, contemplating the sea incarnadined, the ruby glow on the Princes' Islands, and the faint amethyst of the Asian mainland culminating in the snows of the Bithynian Olympus."[33]

Lucy Garnett:

"One of the predominating instincts of the Osmanli Turks has ever been a passion for the picturesque in nature, a love of splendid sites, sparkling seas, leafy shades, cool fountains, and wide horizons; and this instinct has led them, wherever they have settled, to choose for their abodes the most charming situations, commanding views unrivalled in grandeur and beauty."[34]

Miss Julia Pardoe:

"The day of rest and recreation levels all ranks, and suspends all distinctions; and thus each is secure to find the pleasure which he seeks; for that pleasure is in itself of so natural and

simple a description that it requires no combination of causes to produce it—a bright sky, a balmy atmosphere, a lovely landscape—are all that is necessary to its enjoyment; and they are ever within the reach of the humblest during the long summer season. And when to these are superadded the kindly smile and the ready greeting which are never withheld in Turkey from those who seek them, it must at once be acknowledged that the Osmanlis have made a wise selection, in preferring to the strife and struggle for precedence, and the uncertainty of ultimate success, which clog the more refined and 'exclusive' pleasures of Europe, the simple, kindly, and ever-enduring enjoyment of nature and universal good-will.

"But I am committing an error in thus applying the word 'refined.' Are not such pleasures as those of Turkey infinitely more refined than the elaborated dissipations of the West? Is not the holiness of nature a loftier contemplation than the gilded saloons of the great? The power to feel and to appreciate the noble gifts of the Creator, eminently more glorious than the talent to discover the finite perfections of the creature? Is not the breeze which sweeps over the heathy hill, or through the blossom-scented valley, more redolent of real sweetness than the perfume-laden halls of luxury?

"If these be 'barbarous' pleasures, then are the Turks the most barbarous people upon earth, for in these consist their highest enjoyments. In them the Minister finds his ready solace for the cares of office, and the labourer for the toils of weary days. But if they be indeed those which should be the best calculated to impart their charm to cultivated minds and unsullied hearts; then, as I have already ventured to suggest, the Turks have 'chosen the better part,' and are authorized to smile, as they ever do, in quiet pity at the coil and care with which we of 'civilized' Europe cheat ourselves into the belief that we have far outstripped them in enjoyment, as well as science; and toil throughout a long life in pursuit of a phantom which flits before us like a beckoning spirit, but is ever beyond our grasp.

"I was never more struck with this truth than at Guiuk-Suy [Göksu]. I never saw the women of Turkey under a more favorable aspect. Every heart appeared to be holding holyday; and when, as evening closed, we returned to our caique, and bade adieu to the valley of the Asian Sweet Waters, I felt that I knew them better—that I understood more correctly their social character—than I had hitherto done."[35]

33

Social Status

Edmondo de Amicus:

"The Turk is kind and just toward his family. He is generally more respectful of marriage and family ties than are Europeans. Although it is always stated to the contrary, women's status among Muslims is not lower than that of Christian women in Europe. Women have absolute sovereignty in their houses and are always treated kindly and courteously."[36]

La Baronne Durand de Fontmagne:

"Turkish women are usually treated with the refinement of a chevalier. No one would attempt to raise a hand against a woman. Even during times of rebellion and disorder, no soldier would touch a loud and boisterous woman. Men behave like a very polite friend to their wives. Their respect toward their mothers is infinite."[37]

A. L. Castellan:

"Turks are extremely respectful to women. They consider it a sin to stare at women in public places."[38]

Lady Craven:

"The treatment of Turkish women should be an example for all nations."[39]

M. de M. D'Ohsson:

"Anyone who behaves badly towards a woman, regardless of his position or religion, cannot escape punishment, because religion generally commands women to be respected. For this reason both the police and judges deal very severely with anyone who ill-treats women."[40]

◀ Rogier, *Drapers in the Covered Bazaar*, 1848

II

Ottoman Women in the Household Harem

*W*omen are not prisoners in any sense of the word, nor are they pining behind their latticed windows as we are sometimes led to believe... This seclusion does not rest heavily upon Mohammedan women, and she would be the first to resent the breaking of her seclusion... as showing that she had lost value in her husband's eyes.[41]

Elizabeth Cooper, 1916

◀ Osman Hamdi, *Dressing Up*

◀ Ottoman house interior, Istanbul

The Myth

For centuries the harem myth has immensely influenced the minds of Westerners. According to the myth, Ottoman women (Oriental women in general) were indolent, erotic and untrustworthy. They were depicted in both words and pictures as sex objects whose main purpose of existence was to provide pleasure for the male libido. This stereotype was typically represented in paintings of the female slave or odalisque (*odalık* in Turkish), drawn as an exotic nude reclining on a sofa awaiting the amorous attentions of her master. Sensual scenes of nude females lounging in the Turkish *hamam* (public bath) were also popular expressions of this stereotype. At the same time, Ottoman women were portrayed as pitiable victims, creatures captive in the harem without any individual agency. They were described as suppressed and constrained by a life of imprisonment in the confines of the harem.

The origin of this myth lies in the work of the early Orientalist scholars, one of the most famous of which is the translation of the *Thousand and One Nights*. First printed in French during 1707–1714 and then in several different English versions, this imaginary and exotic account of the harem became immensely popular in the West. Its great success set off a literary trend, and this work was followed by the publication of many more oriental and pseudo-oriental tales. The popularity of *The Arabian*

Lewis, *The Reception*, 1873

Nights is significant because the female stereotypes it conjured up became the template for Westerners' perception of Ottoman women. On the one hand, we have a stereotype of lewd and deceitful women behaving indecently in the tales, and, on the other hand, in the narrator Sheherezad we have a pure and sexually neutral female *persona*.

These female stereotypes were not new but only took on a more exotic hue in regard to Oriental women. These polarized images of women had long existed in Western men's consciousness. However, we cannot trace them back to the ancient Greeks. There was no stigma on female sexuality in the Greek myths. Both goddesses and mortal women freely exercised their sexuality without being condemned for it. In Greek art as well, female sexuality as represented in the physical form is elevated to a plane of beauty and perfection. It inspires admiration and awe, not lust and desire. Turning to the Christian tradition, however, we get a very different perspective. The images become polarized. Women are either pure like the Virgin Mary or "fallen" like Mary Magdalene. Virginity is seen as a prerequisite for spiritual purity, and thus we find many early Christians, men and women, living a life of celibacy. Sexuality is seen, at best, as a necessary evil for procreation, and for many men and women of the Catholic Church, celibacy has remained a mandatory and accepted way of life over the centuries.

In view of these parameters regarding female sexuality, it is not difficult to understand why Western males put Oriental women in the erotic or "fallen" category. After all, until the mid-eighteenth century they put most Western women in that category as well. It was only in the nineteenth century that domestic Victorian married women were allowed in the category of "respectable" women, but only at the cost of being "the angel in the house,"[42] who endured the evil of sexual activity only for the sake of having children. Many Victorian men, on the other hand, indulged their sexual fantasies with prostitutes who were more enjoyable partners than their "angelic" wives. This led to a double social standard that condoned the promiscuity of "respectable" men, but which condemned female infidelity.

The Western male's traditional polarized images of women plus the exotic tales of oriental females combined to make a strong case for the myth of the harem. In addition to these, normally no foreign men were ever permitted to enter an Ottoman harem, so there

Van Loo, *Eunuchs Serving the Sultan*, 1772–1773

were no eye-witness reports to contradict the myth. Male travelers cited other male writers, whose information was often based on hearsay or their own fantasies. The truth was often stretched or partially presented, and, at times, there were outright lies. A case in point is the handkerchief story, according to which the sultan supposedly dropped a handkerchief in front of the *cariye* (slave girl) he wanted to invite to his bed. After being bathed and perfumed, the *cariye* supposedly crept into the foot of the sultan's bed. This story was repeated again and again by male travelers, although they had no corroboration of it. It was not until Western women traveled to the Ottoman Empire and saw Ottoman harems and the women in them first hand, that more realistic descriptions of harem life became available.

Lady Montague played a key role in initiating a more realistic discourse on Ottoman women and harem life. She was the first renowned female traveler to the Ottoman Empire who reported more realistic descriptions of women in the harem to her readers. In a letter to Lady Rich she wrote the following criticism regarding the unreliability of male travelers' accounts:

"Your whole letter is full of mistakes from one end to the other. I see you have taken your ideas of Turkey from that worthy author Dumont, who has wrote with equal ignorance and confidence. It is a particular pleasure to me here, to read the voyages to the Levant, which are generally so far removed from the truth, and so full of absurdities, I am very well diverted with them. They never fail giving you an account of the women, whom it is certain they never saw, and talking very wisely of the genius of men, into whose company they are never admitted; and very often describe mosques, which they dare not even peep into."[43]

It was Lady Montague who debunked the handkerchief story. During her visit to Hafize, the former favorite consort of the deceased Sultan Mustafa, who had died a few weeks after being deposed from the throne, Montague was told that the tale of the handkerchief and creeping into the bed was totally untrue. To the contrary, the sultan's consorts were first informed of the sultan's pleasure by the *kahya kadın* (chief housekeeper) who had learned of it from the *kızlar ağası*, the chief black eunuch, who had been informed by the sultan, himself. Also the sultan was bound by etiquette to visit his concubines in strict order. The first in line was the *Kadın* (consort) he had first favored, then the second, and so on. A consort lost her turn only when she was indisposed for some reason. Montague goes on to normalize the sultan's actions by comparing his behavior to that of European monarchs:

"Sometimes the sultan diverts himself in the company of all his ladies, who stand in a circle around him. And she (Hafize) confessed, they were ready to die with envy and jealousy of the happy she that he distinguished by any appearance of preference. But this seemed to me neither better nor worse than the circles in most courts, where the glance of the monarch is watched, and every smile is waited for with impatience, and envied by those who cannot obtain it."[44]

In addition to Lady Montague, there were a number of nineteenth-century female travelers like Julia Pardoe, Lucy Garnett and Fanny Blunt who continued to normalize the harem and the women in it by describing them realistically rather than exotically. In the writings of these Western women they focused on every kind of detail: the harem furnishings, the women's dress and manners, the food they ate, the slaves and how they were treated, the children and how they were cared for, visits to the public baths, outings, religious rituals, holidays, and so on—all were dealt with at length and in great detail. Having examined the lives of Ottoman women at close hand, many Western women no longer saw Ottoman women either as exotic creatures or as captives in the harem.

Victorian female travelers not only divested the harem of its negative images as a nest of eroticism and a prison for Ottoman women, which Western Orientalists and male travelers had given it previously, but they actually praised it as a sacred sphere for women, separate from the profane public sphere of men. Now it was claimed that women were secluded in the harem because their husbands valued and respected them so much, not because their husbands were suppressing them. Women were seen as sacred personages who must be protected from the common multitudes:

"The seclusion of the Harem appears to be no more than the natural wish of the husband to guard his beloved from even the knowledge of the ills and woes that mortal man betides... he wishes to protect 'his lady bird' 'the light of his Harem' from all trouble and anxiety... as we carefully enshrine a valuable gem or protect a sacred relic from the profane gaze of the multitude, so does he on the same principle hide from the vulgar kin his best... The Turks, in their gallantry, consider the person of a woman sacred, and the place of her retreat, her haram, is always respected."[45]

Perhaps it would be more accurate to say that Ottoman men and women recognized both the sacred as well as the physical natures of women.

The Ka'ba, Mecca

Sacred Space

The word *harem*, stemming from the Arabic root *h-r-m*, does, in fact, mean "sacred" or "forbidden," but it does not pertain only to a female space. The sacred cities of Mecca and Medina are referred to by Muslims as the *Haremeyn-i Şerifeyn*. The Aqsa Mosque in Jerusalem is called the Noble Sanctuary or *Harem-i Şerif*. Also, in Ottoman usage the inner courtyard of a mosque was a harem.[46] When Topkapı Palace was newly built during the reign of Fatih Sultan Mehmed (the Conqueror), the women and children of the royal household were still living in the Old Palace. Even though the new palace was only inhabited by males at that time, the inner precinct of the palace or the sultan's living quarters were known as the imperial harem or *Harem-i Hümayûn* because of the sultan's presence there. The term *harem* is one of respect

Calligraphic panel, 1849: "Allah, may His Glory be exalted; Muhammad, peace be upon him"

and is "redolent of religious purity and honor, and evocative of the requisite obeisance."[47]

The word *harem* also designates the living quarters of females in a domestic residence and the women living there as well. In addition, at the beginning of the twentieth century it was used to designate women's compartments in railway trains, ladies' waiting rooms at train stations and space reserved for them on steamers and tramcars.[48] In general, access to the female harem is forbidden to males, except that in domestic harems this ban does not apply to a woman's immediate male relatives which include her husband, father, uncles, brothers, sons and father-in-law. In Ottoman society respect for the female harem and the

Ottoman *yali* (seaside house) on the Bosphorous, 18th century

Catenacci, *Amcazade Hüseyin Paşa Yalısı (Köprülü) Divanhanesi*, 1863

women living in it was strictly observed by males publicly and privately. Many Western female travelers comment upon the fact that an Ottoman woman's husband would not think of intruding into his own harem if he saw women's slippers at the harem door, a sign that there were female guests in the harem.

Incense burner, 1885
Topkapı Palace

Physical Space

Ottoman houses were divided into two sections: the *selamlık* and *haremlik*. The *selamlık* was the room or rooms where the man of the house received male visitors, who were served by male slaves. The *haremlik* was the part of the house where the husband lived with his wife, children and any other female relatives he was taking care of. They were attended by female slaves. The harems were usually described as spacious and sparsely furnished rooms. There would be a large anteroom (*sofa*) in the middle with smaller rooms branching off from it. The anteroom was where much of the social interaction took place. The lady of the house, her children, female

47

Mustafa Paşa Kiosk, Topkapı Palace

Wall recess. Baghdad Kiosk,
Topkapı Palace

relatives, female slaves and female guests all socialized here.
Meals were usually eaten here and in some homes beds were
spread in this room at night for sleeping. The rooms were usually
multi-functional. That is, they were used for different purposes
rather than having a specific purpose such as dining, sitting or
sleeping.

Furnishings usually consisted of built-in sofas, which were
wooden platforms raised off the floor, often on three sides of the
room. Large cushions covered with rich materials (according
to the means of the home owner) were placed on these raised
platforms and formed the seating space used by both family

members and guests. The fourth wall often contained a large cupboard where bedding was stored during the day and a few shelf niches where water pitchers, rose-water ewers or other household items were placed. Curtains and carpets completed the furnishings. Although the furnishings were sparse, the rooms were attractive with painted and gilded ceilings and many windows allowing for abundant light. In the homes of the wealthy, marble fountains were sometimes found in the anterooms, and the fabrics used were made from rich material like silk and brocade in elegant designs. At meal time large round trays were brought into the anteroom by slaves and placed upon a small portable base. Cushions were put around the trays where family members or guests sat for the meal. Slaves carried in and out various dishes of food and then collected the trays again after the meal was over. The houses were heated in the winter by a brazier called *tandır*. It resembled a short round table in which hot ashes were put and was covered with a large cloth, often cashmere. People would sit around it with their feet under the table and much of their bodies under the cover in order to keep warm. They would socialize, work, read and sometimes even sleep at the *tandır*.

The following first-hand description of an Ottoman house is given by Lady Montague. She describes the house in Edirne where she and her husband, the British ambassador, lodged when they came to the Ottoman Empire in 1717:

"Every house, great and small, is divided into two distinct parts, which only join together by a narrow passage. The first house ... is the house belonging to the lord, and the adjoining one is called the harem, that is, the ladies' apartment ... it has also a gallery running around it towards the garden, to which all the windows are turned, and the same number of chambers as the other, but more gay and splendid, both in painting and furniture. The second row of windows is very low, with grates like those of convents; the rooms are all spread with Persian carpets, and raised at one end (my chamber is raised at both ends) about two feet. This is the sofa, and is laid with a richer sort of carpet, and

all around it a sort of couch, raised half a foot, covered with rich silk according to the fancy or magnificence of the owner. Mine is of scarlet cloth, with a gold fringe; round this are placed, standing against the wall, two rows of cushions, the first very large, and the next little ones; and here the Turks display their greatest magnificence. They are generally brocade, or embroidery of gold wire upon white satin—nothing can look more gay and splendid. These seats are so convenient and easy, I shall never endure chairs as long as I live. The rooms are low, which I think is no fault, and the ceiling is nearly always of wood, generally inlaid or painted and gilded. They use no hangings, the rooms being all wainscoated with cedar set off with silver nails or painted with flowers, which open in many places with folding doors, and serve for cabinets, I think, more conveniently than ours. Between the windows are little arches to set pots of perfume, or baskets of flowers. But what pleases me best is the fashion of having marble fountains in the lower part of the room, which throw up several spouts of water, giving at the same time an agreeable coolness, and a pleasant dashing sound, falling from one basin to another. Some of these fountains are very magnificent. Each house has a bagnio, which is generally two or three little rooms, leaded at the top, paved with marble, with basins, cocks of water, and all conveniences for either hot or cold baths."[49]

A more detailed first-hand account of a Turkish harem is given by Lucy Garnett:

"The larger division of the house constitutes the 'haremlik,' which has its separate entrance, courtyard and garden, and contains all the private apartments of the family. As in the generality of Eastern houses, the front door opens into a large hall, which gives access to rooms on each side of it, and has several windows at the opposite end. One of these rooms is the 'kahve-ocak,' or 'coffee-hearth,' where an old woman may always be found presiding over a charcoal brazier ready to boil coffee at a moment's notice; the others are storerooms and sleeping apartments

Preziosi, *Spice-seller*, 1861

of the inferior slaves. The kitchen, which is very spacious, is generally an out-building. One side of it is occupied by the great arched cooking-stove with its numerous little grates, on which the contents of brightly burnished copper pans simmer over charcoal fires, fanned with a turkey's wing by the negress cook. A wide staircase leads from the entrance floor to the upper hall, the centre of which is generally occupied by a spacious ante-room, on which other apartments open. In some of the older houses the 'divan-khane,' or principal reception room, contains a large alcove, the floor of which is raised about a foot above the level of the rest of the apartment. A low divan furnishes its three sides, and its most comfortable corner is the 'hanum's' habitual seat. If the 'divan-khane' has not such a recess, one end and half the two adjoining wings of the room are usually occupied by a continuous sofa, and the fourth is furnished with a marble-topped console table surmounted by a mirror and candelabra, and flanked on either side by shelves in niches, containing rose-water sprinklers, sherbet goblets, and other ornamental objects. A few European chairs stand stiffly against the wall in every space left vacant and one or two walnut tray-stools, inlaid with mother-of-pearl, are placed near the divan to hold cigarettes, ash-trays, matches, coffee-cups and other trifles. A few framed 'yaftas,' or texts from the Koran, may be seen on the walls, but pictures are, generally, conspicuous by their absence...

"Bedsteads are not used by old-fashioned Turks. Each room contains a large cupboard, built into the wall, in which the bedding is piled during the day, and at night the slaves come in, when summoned, to make up the beds on the floor. Other bedroom furniture in the shape of washstands, dressing-tables, and wardrobes is dispensed with as superfluous. For everyday ablutions there is a small washing-room with a hole in the floor for the water to escape through, and when it is proposed to wash the hands and face only, a slave brings in the 'leğen' [basin] and 'ibrik' [ewer] and pours the water; while, for special ablutions, the private 'hammams' or the public baths will be resorted to. The 'hanum' 'does her hair' or has it done for her, seated cross-legged in

Preziosi, *Confectioner*, 1861

her corner of the divan; and the quaintly carved and painted walnut-wood chests and coffers in her treasure-room suffice to hold her gauzes and brocades, her silks and embroideries."[50]

It can be seen by Lucy Garnett's description of the harem, which was published in 1909, that furnishings, for the most part, are still Ottoman in traditional families. Beds (mattresses), for example, are still stored in closets during the day and brought out at night. The rooms are still multi-functional, being used as sitting rooms, dining rooms, bed rooms and living rooms as needed in contrast to Victorian houses where rooms were uni-functional. A few items such as chairs, a console table and mirror are mentioned, indicating that the European influence has begun. The use of European furnishings increased with time, often leading to an eclectic and esthetically displeasing mixture of furniture. After commenting on the beauty and richness of traditional Ottoman carpets, textiles and embroidery, Garnett adds:

"The Oriental mind seems, as a rule, to become confused when it endeavours to assimilate its own notions of luxury and magnificence to those suggested by the civilization of the West. The highest developments of art are brought into close contact with objects of the most tasteless construction, and magnificence is thrown into strong and unpleasing relief by juxtaposition with tawdriness; ... shabby chintz hangs side by side with rich brocade and velvet; and a cheap rug "made in Germany," and representing a dog or lion, is spread side by side with a silken carpet of almost priceless value."[51]

Social Space / Social Roles

Ottoman household harems were very social and gregarious places. Here all the women and young children of the house lived and worked together. This often included the mother-in-law, particularly if she was widowed, and sometimes other elderly women such as aunts, the wife, her young children and numerous female slaves. Large harems of the Ottoman elite were known to have as many as a hundred slaves to perform the daily household tasks. In addition, female friends, relatives, neighbors, vendors and singers were always welcome to drop in. Emine Fuat Tugay writes that in her childhood (b.1897) place settings for sixteen were laid every day at lunch and that there were rarely any empty places. She, two brothers, her mother and their two governesses took up six seats, while the rest were left for unexpected guests.[52] Women of all ages, races and social status mingled in the harems, but a strict etiquette was in force at all times. The mistress of the house and distinguished guests sat on the sofa, while women of lower social status sat on cushions on the floor. The democratic nature of the harems is summarized by Tugay as follows:

"Whatever their status everyone was well received, according to the old Ottoman tradition. That period represents the last stages of a patriarchal hospitality, and was in actual fact a truly democratic system in the only genuine meaning of the word, since persons of every class had access to and were made welcome by the highest in the land. Good manners among all classes were the rule. A woman of inferior rank would never presume to sit close to the mistress of the house, but when asked to be seated, would of her own accord choose a chair placed at some distance from her hostess. Women of humbler condition sat near the door, on stiff cushions placed on the floor for that purpose. But all, whenever they wished to come, had the satisfaction of being admitted to the presence of even the greatest ladies in the land."[53]

Role of Mother-in-law

If she lived with her son, the *kayın valide* [the bride's mother-in-law] was at the top of the social hierarchy in the household harem, similar to the role of the sultan's mother, the *valide sultan*, in the imperial harem. The mother-in-law in both the imperial and household harems was always held in the highest esteem and was shown great respect by other harem members. This privileged position can be traced to the command in the Holy Qur'an to "Reverence the wombs,"[54] a command that the Ottomans fully honored. The mother-in-law had the final say in all matters related to the harem, and she oversaw its daily operations. The following excerpts from Western travelers' reports underscore the importance of the mother-in-law's role in the Ottoman household harem:

"The chief personage in the harem is the husband's mother, and owing to the patriarchal custom of married children living under the parental roof, she is more frequently a member of the household than are mothers-in-law with us. She takes precedence of the wife, and as long as she lives is the 'buyuk hanum,' the great lady of the house. The utmost deference is paid to her."[55]

"If a man's widowed mother reside permanently under his roof, which is not unusual, his wife's position in the house is but secondary, and she is required to defer to her mother-in-law in all things. Hand-kissing being the usual mode of respectful greeting, the wife kisses the

hand of her 'Kain Valide,' [mother-in-law] as also that of her husband, on the occasion of any family event, or any anniversary, and also on special Moslem holidays, such as the opening of the Bairam [eid] festival. The wife may not seat herself at table before her husband's mother has taken her place, nor be the first to help herself to the dishes, nor may she smoke a cigarette in the presence of 'the first lady' until invited by her to do so."[56]

Role of Wife

In the absence of the husband's mother, the wife was the head of the Ottoman household harem. She had full authority over the running of daily activities, the harem economy, female slaves and child-rearing. This was often no small task due to the size of some harems, particularly those of the elite. However, young girls were trained for these duties from childhood on. By the time they married, they had learned the skills necessary for successfully running a household. The harem became the arena in which women could display their talents and ingenuity. Marriage, and motherhood in particular, gave them respect and security both in the family and in society at large.

As mentioned previously, girls were trained for their role as wife and mother at an early age. They attended a primary school (*sıbyan mektebi*) where they learned basic Islamic knowledge such as the Arabic alphabet, recitation of the Qur'an and memorization of some of its verses, catechism, the proper performance of ritual prayers, writing, arithmetic, geography and history. These schools were usually attached to a mosque and they were in existence for centuries. They were also widespread. Western travelers wrote that there was no village too small to have a primary school.

In 1858 the first girls' secondary school was opened in Istanbul. By 1901 the number of these schools in Istanbul had increased to eleven. Classes were held every day except for Friday during ten months of the year. There were thirty-six hours of lessons per week and eighteen different subjects. The broad curriculum included the Alphabet and Verbal Studies, the Holy Qur'an and Rules of Recitation, Religious Studies, Reading, Writing, Literature, Ottoman Grammar, Arabic, Persian, Calligraphy, General Information about Life, Household Management, Ethics, Health, Arithmetic-Geometry, Geography, History and Handcrafts.

Lewis, *School*, c. 1850

In addition to offering a broad curriculum, these schools taught detailed information regarding household management that prepared young girls for the responsibilities they would face when they married. This is obvious from the following topic headings in the course on Household Management:

What is a home? What things are necessary in order for a house to be called a home? How can it be set up, protected, heated, aired and lighted? The characteristics of a good home; arranging furniture; inner divisions; sanitary conditions; the characteristics of furniture; conditions and solutions for cleaning and protecting the kitchen and other rooms, the bath and ablutions cabin, furniture suites, chairs, cushions, curtains, rug and bedding; cleaning copper,

Frères, *Sultan Ahmed middle school for girls*

bronze, marble and jewelry; solutions for getting rid of bugs, flies, bedbugs, fleas and lice; the characteristics of summer and winter rooms; information about fuel; setting up and cleaning stoves and fireplaces; lighting means: resinous wood, candles, olive oil, liquid gas, natural gas, lamps, candlesticks and night light (small kerosene lamp).

Protecting clothing in different seasons; sewing; weaving underwear; weaving carpets and rugs; information about looms; cleaning clothes with lime water, soda and soap; starching and ironing; removing stains; embroidery; needlework; different kinds of covers.

Making bread; yeast; preserving food in different seasons; drying fresh vegetables and fruit in season; making pickles, jams, syrup, braised meat, pastrami-sausages, plain foods and those made with olive oil, pastries, compotes; pantries; and determining minimum weekly consumption of basic foods according to the number of family members.

Home pharmacy: Making tooth powder and water and creams for chapped hands and lips; natural and

Frères, *Students of a private school,* 1880–1893 ▶

57

artificial toothbrushes; bath luffas; wash cloths and bathrobes. Introduction to natural herbs and home medicines. Information on bleeding, poisoning, and so on.

Home medical information: Regarding wounds, bruises, sprains, broken bones and burns. Caring for people who have just recovered from illness. Conditions for choosing a family doctor.

Clothing and food for every season; arranging meal times; daily nutrition for children, middle-aged persons and the elderly; sleeping times according to age; daily and weekly cleaning.

Information on keeping the sitting room ready for guests; ...rules of etiquette; customs regarding speaking, serving, respect and love; characteristics of servants; things to be done when staying alone; always being prepared for unexpected guests; being clean and well-kept; visiting rules.

Keeping a daily accounts notebook; making a monthly budget; making savings; being respectful of rental conditions if renting; and keeping up the home whether owner or renter.[57]

Whether educated at school or in the home, young Ottoman girls were well-prepared for taking up their responsibilities in the household harem. They were equipped with the knowledge and experience necessary for their wifely roles. In addition to being taught practical knowledge, Ottoman girls and boys were carefully trained in social manners and refinement. There was a strict hierarchy based on seniority in homes and in society, and children of all classes were raised to respect its rules. The younger always showed respect to the elder, and this was the case even among siblings. On the other hand, the older siblings were responsible for the well-being of the younger children.

The role of wife offered the Ottoman woman many benefits including her maintenance, the companionship of a husband, support from her family throughout her life and a secure and respectable place in society. Objective Western travelers overwhelmingly agreed that Ottoman women had full control over their own domains. In fact, some travelers went so far as to say that those who thought otherwise deserved to be laughed at.[58] According to Western travelers' reports, Ottoman women were treated kindly, compassionately and respectfully by their husbands. Western women were particularly impressed by the respect for women's privacy shown by Ottoman men. In general, Ottoman men treated their wives with so much respect and courtesy that Lady Craven suggested the behavior of Turkish men towards their wives should be taken as an example by all nations.

Physical abuse of Muslim women was rare in Ottoman society. Both the law and social mores protected women. Men were forbidden to speak to women on the streets, and it was considered shameful for men even to look directly at women other than their own wives or close female blood relatives. A striking example of this is related by Antoine-Ignace Melling (1763–1831), an architect in the employment of Hatice Sultan, sister to Sultan Selim III. While working on Hatice Sultan's palace, Melling was able to see the female slaves in the palace courtyard. The palace foreman, who accompanied the European architect, always turned his head to avoid seeing the slave girls, saying that God commanded men not to stare at women other than their own.[59] Lady Ramsey gives an interesting anecdote from her own travels regarding male behavior towards females. Although she traveled widely in the Ottoman Empire, she saw only one example of abuse to a woman. In her own words:

"It was a lovely sunny morning, and I was taking a look about, while the men packed up our belongings and my husband made notes of the locality. My attention was attracted by an angry shout from the opposite side of the glen. I looked across and saw a middle-aged man, in peasant garb, shouting and gesticulating violently, and evidently in a very bad temper. He was accompanied by four or five women carrying hoes. I suppose they were going to work in the fields. The man had stopped and turned at the top of a steep road and the women had stopped and turned also. I saw that the angry individual addressed himself to another woman, who was some yards behind, and I made out that he was ordering her to go back to the house. Still farther down the road a wee child, hardly able to walk, was doing its little utmost to overtake the woman.

"While the man roared and gesticulated the woman stood still; but the moment he turned his back to continue his way she slowly followed. When this had happened three or four times, his rage became unbounded, he made a rush at her, lifted her in his two hands high in the air (she was a little bit of a thing), and threw her with all his force against a wall. She did not utter a sound so far as I heard, but lay huddled up and motionless like a bundle of clothes. But the baby, that had by this time almost reached her, lifted up its voice in shrieks of anguish and terror, and the four or five women who were with the man stooped with one accord, each picked up a stone and let fly at him. I think some of them hit him. I sincerely hope they did. He was apparently ashamed of himself, for he took no notice of this action on the part of the women, but walked hastily away leaving them to follow."[60]

The remarkable aspect of this anecdote is not the angry man's abuse of his intractable wife, but the village women's reaction to the man's abuse. They showed neither fear nor abject submission in the face of a male's physical force. They apparently didn't fear for their livelihood either. Their swift reaction to physical force with physical force suggests that they were confident of being morally and legally in the right. Moreover, the lack of any reaction to the women's stone-throwing further suggests that the furious man thought they were in the right, too.

Roles of Mother and Children

Motherhood further enhanced and consolidated the Ottoman wife's position because mothers were revered and honored in Ottoman society. The hadith, "Heaven is under the feet of mothers," indicates the strong religious basis for this attitude. Ottoman women were devoted mothers. They showed great care and tenderness towards their children. Either the mother, herself, saw to the needs of her child or she oversaw the care given by slave women who served as nurses. Many of the activities of child-raising took place in the large anteroom of the harem. Children mixed freely with adults and were included as a natural part of harem activities. This led some Victorian women, who were accustomed to children being kept in totally separate quarters, to conclude that children, both girls and boys, in Ottoman families were overly indulged by their mothers and nurses.

Young boys usually remained with their mothers in the harem until the age of seven, at which time they began to participate in all-male functions in the *selamlık*. Girls remained in the harem until they married and took on the responsibility of running their own households. Both boys and girls were treated with great affection, but mothers were also careful to cultivate refined manners in their children. Due to the seclusion of Ottoman women, they devoted almost all of their time and energy to their husband and children. In turn, children were highly respectful and considerate of their elders. They were particularly devoted to their mothers both in childhood and adulthood. According to Julia Pardoe,

"An equally beautiful feature in the character of the Turks is their reverence and respect for the author of their being ... the mother is an oracle; she is consulted, confided in, listened to with respect and deference, honored to her latest hour, and remembered with affection and regret beyond the grave."[61]

◀ Rogier, *Female Servant Serving Coffee*, 1848

Preziosi, *Caique*, 1858

The strong bonds between parents and children, the devotion and care given by parents to their children when they were young and by the children to their parents in their old age, the refinement of manners and behavior towards all family members, and the solidarity and unity of purpose led to the Ottoman family's being, what one Swiss family-law professor described as, "the strongest family hearth in the world."[62] Of course there were many significant factors that contributed to the success of the Ottoman family. The Ottomans' strict adherence to Islam, their honoring and practicing cultural values, traditions and customs that gave importance to the family, and the support and protection of family values by Ottoman institutions like the neighborhood administration system, guilds, religious organizations and government—all were vital aspects of Ottoman family synergy.

Speaking from her own personal experience as a child born in 1906 into an Ottoman family, Münevver Ayaşlı Hanımefendi said, *"I don't believe that the beauty, purity and sincerity of Ottoman family life have existed anywhere else. The Ottoman Islamic life was life at the pinnacle of beauty. Love and respect towards one another, the visits of the young to their elders on religious holidays, the caresses and compliments from adults to the young—it was truly a life full of poetry. If you ask me what Ottoman life was, I would answer that it was a beautiful, flower-embellished poem."[63]*

Social Activities

The Ottomans were socially oriented people. Just as there was much social interaction among members of the harem, which included daily intermingling of all ages, races and classes of women, there was also a lot of social activity in the harem that included females from outside of the harem. As a society, both Ottoman men and women shared significant events in their lives with others through ceremonies in celebration or commemoration of those events. Births, circumcisions, engagements, marriages and religious holidays were all major events celebrated in accordance with prescribed traditions and customs, and they were experiences shared among relatives, neighbors and friends. In addition, there were many minor events celebrated as well such as the appearance of the baby's first tooth, a child's first day at school, a child's first complete reading of the Qur'an, a young girl's first veiling, a young man's entrance into and return home from the military, an adult's return from the holy pilgrimage, and so on. There were also social events, as well, other than celebrations such as weekly visits to the public baths, visits and return visits, shopping excursions, picnics, and so on. Although Ottoman women were secluded in their harems and basically excluded from the public domain of men, they were in no way confined to a life of loneliness. There was an exclusively female social realm that provided Ottoman women with ample social activity and interaction. This woman's world is described nostalgically below by a ninety-seven-year-old Ottoman woman to her great, great granddaughter in a twentieth century Turkish short story:

"There was a woman's world then, separate from the men, but it's completely vanished today. It was a very wide world. Thousands of women met, spoke with and entertained each other. They had their own special pleasures and amusements. There was no fashion. Young girls wore their mothers' clothing, and grandmothers gave their jewelry to their granddaughters. Silver embroidered slippers, red cloaks... ah, those red cloaks... Women shone like poppies on spring's green grass in excursion places. There were no ugly, that is, weak or sickly ones among them. Men only knew their own women; they came home early from work; and they created scenes of insatiable love and affection for their wives... There were no disaster areas like coffeehouses, casinos, beer halls, clubs, theaters, musical cafes or brothels that separate all Turkish men from their wives and leave miserable Turkish women alone like forgotten keepers in their houses. Women lived with men without worrying. They came together and were amused and happy in those great houses with large halls, in yards with arbors and pools, in gardens, and in huge, unique seaside mansions. What games and customs and pleasures there were then, but they have all been forgotten today...

"Everything was pleasure and fun for us. Everything—childhood, starting school, veiling, marrying, giving birth, even getting old... They all had ceremonies. These events in a woman's life were a vehicle of pleasure and entertainment for many other women. Our whole life passed in pleasure. Not a single week passed without there being a start to school, a circumcision, a wedding, a visit to a mother after childbirth. Our clothing and henna were even a reason for amusement. We had poems and songs. We would get together and consult among one another. On winter evenings we looked for good omens; even the seasons were a source of entertainment for us. Each season had its own customs, amusements and traditions."[64]

Weddings

One of the most important events in the life of an Ottoman woman was, of course, her wedding. Since marriages were arranged, the marriage process began with a visit to the eligible girl's home by the prospective groom's mother and sometimes a matchmaker, who might be a relative, friend, neighbor or a professional matchmaker. The purpose of the visit was for the prospective mother-in-law to see the girl at close range. Once the visitors were seated in the best room and the young girl had dressed for the occasion, she would serve Turkish coffee to the guests. While slowly sipping her coffee, the mother of the prospective groom carefully but discreetly looked the girl over. As soon as the coffee drinking was finished, the young girl would collect the empty cups on a tray and withdraw from the room.

If the woman approved of the girl, she would inform her husband, and son and the family would arrive at a decision. If it was positive, the boy's father and several male relatives called on the girl's father and asked for the bridal candidate's hand in marriage. Before giving an answer, the girl's father would have investigated the character and resources of the boy's family, if he did not know them already. This time, the girl's family decided whether or not to accept the marriage proposal. If the family agreed and if the girl gave her consent, then the go-ahead was given by the girl's father. A number of visits between the two families ensued. Terms of the marriage were discussed and agreed upon and gifts were exchanged during these visits.

One of the most important points discussed between the two parties was the amount of the *mahr* to be paid to the bride. Unlike a dowry (which a bride brings with her to the marriage) or a bride price (which goes to the father of the bride), the *mahr* is a sum of money or property paid or promised by the groom to the bride. It is a mandatory condition of marriage in Islam, and the marriage should not be consummated until the terms of the *mahr* have been agreed upon and the necessary payment made. During Ottoman times one part of the *mahr* was paid before the marriage and one part was left to be paid in case of divorce or death of the husband. It is both a means of financial security for the woman in case of divorce or death, and it is also a deterrent to divorce for the man. The amount of *mahr* was usually determined in correlation with the bride's social status.

When all terms had been agreed upon between the two families, the couple became engaged. The bride's family sent a large bundle of gifts to the groom's family, which included sweets and presents for the groom and all members of the immediate family. If the girl's family had the means to do so, gifts could be included for extended family members as well. In turn, the groom's family sent an even more elaborate engagement set of gifts and food to the bride's family, described as follows by Fanny Blunt:

"The 'nişan takımı' [engagement set sent by the groom's family] *was usually much more elaborate than the 'nişan bohçası'* [bundle of gifts sent by the bride's family] *and, among the rich, consisted of five trays carried on the heads of five servants. The first tray contained handsome 'çitpit,' or house slippers, for the bride and for her female relatives, and 'terlik,' less elegant slippers, for her family's servants; a silver hand-mirror; perfumes in tiny crystal bottles; and a filigree silver box, or 'çekmece,' in which lay the 'nişan yüzüğü,' the ring that would serve as both engagement and wedding ring. It was usually set with a single large emerald, ruby, or diamond. The second tray carried flowers; the third baskets of fruit; the fourth baskets of sweets and spices, coffee,*

Melling, *Turkish Wedding Parade*, 1819

colored wax candles, and bags of Mecca henna. On the fifth were the material for the wedding dress and other fabrics, a pair of handsome 'nalın' (clogs) inlaid with mother-of-pearl and equipped with pearl-embroidered straps, a small silver basin, and some elaborate combs for the bride's bath. These trays were each tied in muslin and decorated with ribbons."[65]

At a later appointed date the official marriage ceremony took place at the bride's home in the presence of the *imam*, the male parents or guardians of the bride and groom and male witnesses. A marriage contract was signed between the two parties, containing any conditions the bride and groom wanted specified like the amount of the *mahr*. The bride followed the ceremony in an adjacent room and the groom might be there in person or be represented by someone. The official ceremony was followed by a dinner attended by both parties.

The wedding ceremonies, the social celebration of the couple's marriage, followed the official ceremony at an appointed time. The marriage was consummated on Thursday night, and events preceding this night took place on a traditional timetable. On the Monday preceding the wedding night the bride's trousseau was taken in a procession to the groom's home and displayed there by her female relatives and friends for the curiosity and admiration of relatives and neighbors or any other female visitors. The bride's mother would begin to prepare her daughter's trousseau shortly after she was born. Later, when the girl was capable enough, she, too, would contribute to the preparation of the trousseau, which would usually include:

Bruyn,
Women's Turbans, 1700

"*...numerous silver trays, bowls, and pitchers. In the nineteenth century, it also contained vases made of* çeşm-i bülbül *(nightingale's eyes), a type of colored glass marked by spiral white stripes; tulip vases called* lâledan; *crystal bowls; household items ornamented with* sırma, *an embroidery done with gold or silver thread, in this case much of it by the bride's own hand; jewels protected by glass; two* oda takımları, *that is, sets of furniture for two rooms—such things as braziers, inlaid mother-of-pearl stools, rugs, and fringed* makats, *divan covers, of the same material as the pillows and window curtains, in most instances a* sırmalı *red velvet; kitchen, eating, and ablution utensils. Even the dustpans were elaborate—of walnut inlaid with silver. There might be as many as fifty sets of bedding. And, of course, there was the girl's wardrobe, which consisted of everything from* geceliks *(nightgowns) to* yaşmaks *(veils), much of it embroidered with* sırma *by the bride.*"[66]

The trousseau items would be attractively displayed in the rooms designated for the new couple. The rooms were elaborately decorated and in one corner the women and girls would make a canopy from beautiful materials and embroideries under which the bride would later sit like a queen during the wedding festivities to receive both her husband and her female guests.

The public bath was the scene of celebrations on Tuesday. The bride would be taken there with great ceremony. Her female relatives and friends would attend the traditional bridal bath, the expenses of which were borne by the groom. The bride was thoroughly soaped, scrubbed, shampooed and perfumed by bath attendants, and her hair was braided and adorned with jewels and gold coins. She then proceeded to the cooling room where the guests were waiting. She kissed the hands of the elderly and received the congratulations of all the ladies there. Entertainment was provided by female musicians, singers and dancers, and the bride would follow the entertainment seated on her bridal throne which was adorned with gauze and ribbons. Refreshments were served to all the guests. After the bridal bath it was custom for the girl to dress in borrowed clothes, which she wore until she put on her wedding dress.[67]

Şerbet mahraması. Fruit drink kerchief

On Wednesday afternoon the female relatives of the bridegroom paid a visit to the home of the bride. The bride's mother and female friends met them at the door and escorted them upstairs to a sitting room. There they were served refreshments such as sherbet and Turkish coffee. Shortly thereafter the bride would appear, still dressed in borrowed clothes, escorted by two women who had not been married more than once. After kissing the hand of her mother-in-law, the bride would kiss the hands of the other women there and then sit a few minutes next to her mother-in-law. As a token of affection, they would exchange pieces of candy from which each had taken a bite. After being entertained for some time by musicians and dancing girls, the mother-in-law and her party would take their leave, being invited to the henna festivities that evening. The bride would escort her mother-in-law and guests to the door where she would be showered with small coins by the guests. Children and beggars would wait close to the door to get their share of money that was always distributed at wedding events.

That evening the *kına gecesi* (night of henna), which is a kind of farewell to girlhood, took place. Lucy Garnett described it as follows:

"*When the company are again assembled in the evening, a taper is handed to each of the younger members of the party, who, led by the bride and escorted by the musicians and dancing girls, descend to the garden. Winding in a long and wavy line, now between the fragrant flower-beds, and now in the shadow of the trees and shrubs, their rich dresses, bright jewels, fair faces, and floating hair fitfully lighted by the flickering tapers, their feet moving to the rhythm of the tinkling castanets and wild strains of the dusky-hued Gypsy girls, one might imagine them a troop of Peris engaged in their nocturnal revels. Returning to the house, the bride, divested of her gay attire, enters the reception-room, holding her left arm across her brow, and seats herself on a stool in the center of the apartment. The fingers of her right hand are then covered thickly with henna paste, on which the bridegroom's mother sticks a gold coin, the other guests following suit. This hand, covered with a silken bag, is now held across her face, while the left hand is similarly plastered and decorated by the bride's mother and friends. When the maiden's toes have been similarly treated, the ceremony is terminated with a wild pantomimic dance by the Gypsy performers, at the conclusion of which these women fall into exaggerated postures before the principal ladies in order to receive their guerdon, which is looked for as much from the guests as from the hostess. The bride is then left to repose until the henna is considered to have stained her fingers to the requisite amber hue, when it is washed off.*"[68]

On Thursday morning the bride finally put on her wedding finery, which was heavily adorned with gold or silver thread and pearls. She wore a silk gauze blouse and silk *şalvar* pants under an elaborately embroidered velvet dress, usually of a dark red color. One of the most beautiful embroidery designs was the *bindallı* (one thousand branches) in which the dress is almost covered with an elegant branch motif. The bride also wore beautiful jewelry that usually included gold, pearls, diamonds and other precious stones. Her hair was braided into small braids with silver tinsel strands intertwined, and she wore a large veil that hung down over her dress. Her head cover might also include a silver ornamented headpiece or a short fez ornamented with gold coins or, if from a wealthy family, a crown studded with jewels.

When her adornment was complete, it was custom for the bride to appear before her father who would tie a "bridal girdle" consisting of a metal belt or fine shawl around the waist of his daughter, who would kiss his hand for the last time as a member of his household.[69] After this ceremony the bride would be escorted by the groom's family to her new home. The wedding procession was a colorful affair with men on horseback and women in carriages. The bride was accompanied by a female relative called a *yenge* who would help the new couple get acquainted. The procession would occasionally be interrupted by people on the street who expected some gold coins before getting out of the way, knowing that it was customary for money to be distributed at this time.

The groom was not a part of the wedding procession; rather he waited at the door of his family home to welcome the new bride when she arrived. Once the bridal procession reached its destination, the groom and the *yenge* escorted the bride to the bridal chamber, which had been previously decorated for this occasion. Here the groom had a few minutes alone with the bride for the first time in his residence and, if he was successful in raising the veil, he might get what was often his first opportunity to see the bride's face. Then the groom went to attend to his male guests and the female guests, bringing gifts, entered the bridal chamber to see the bride and examine her trousseau.

Male and female guests were hosted, fed and entertained in separate areas of the house, the men in the *selamlık* and the women in the harem, until the evening prayer. At that time the groom and his guests went to a mosque for prayer. Upon returning home, the groom was sent to the bridal chamber amidst good wishes. The *yenge* led him inside the room where his bride was waiting. If he had not previously lifted his bride's veil, he did so now and presented her with a gift for being able to view her face. The *yenge* left them alone while she prepared them a light dinner. After dinner they were left alone for the night, but the *yenge* stayed close by in case her assistance was needed. The wedding festivities continued for two more days with feasting and visiting.

Ottoman society held the feminine in high esteem, and this was particularly apparent in the traditions and ceremonies surrounding weddings. Throughout the wedding celebration, the bride was the focal point of attention and activity. She was treated like a queen, and her every activity was attended by ceremony and celebration. Even her bath and the application of henna were social occasions shared with other women. The sending of the trousseau and the claiming of the bride were activities accompanied by public processions. The bride's passage from girlhood to marriage was an event shared and celebrated by family and friends, and strangers as well. Ottoman brides received support, prayers and good wishes from the whole community, a powerfully positive note on which to begin a new cycle in life.

Childbirth

A wife's entrance into motherhood was another event elaborately celebrated in Ottoman society. Subsequent births were celebrated as well, but the first birth was particularly significant. The new mother gave birth to her child sitting in a birthing chair, which was a special chair with a high back and arms but the bottom of which had been mostly carved out to facilitate the birth. She would be attended by an experienced midwife who would help with the delivery. Once the child was born, the women present would proclaim the *şehadet* (the Muslim declaration of faith) and the midwife would cut the umbilical cord and swaddle the baby in muslin cloth. The new mother, called *lohusa*, would recline on a divan specially decorated for this occasion. It was covered with richly embroidered pillowcases and sheets and satin or velvet-covered quilts. A Qur'an would hang in an embroidered bag at the head of the bed for protection from the evil eye. Later, the father would be called in to chant the *ezan* (call to prayer) and *şehadet* in the baby's right ear and *bismillah* in its left ear. He would also pronounce the baby's name three times.

If the new mother was feeling up to it, a celebration of the birth with family and friends would be held on the third day. Julia Pardoe described a birth celebration in these words:

"Long before I reached [the hanım's apartment], I was deafened with the noise which issued from its door; the voices of the singing women, the rattle of tambourines, the laughter of the guests, the shouts of the attendant slaves, the clatter of the coffee and sherbet cups, I could scarcely believe I was ushered into a sick chamber...

"Directly opposite to the door stood the bed of the Hanoum the curtains had been withdrawn, and a temporary canopy formed of cachemire shawls arranged in festoons, and linked together with bathing scarfs of gold and silver tissue; and, as the lady was possessed of fifty, which could not all be arranged with proper effect in so limited a space, a silk cord had been stretched along the ceiling to the opposite extremity of the apartment, over which the costly drapery was continued. Fastened to the shawls were head-dresses of coloured gauze, flowered or striped with gold and silver, whence depended oranges, lemons, and candied fruits. Two coverlets of wadded pink satin were folded at the bed's foot; and a sheet of striped crape hung to the floor, where it terminated in a deep fringe of gold.

"The infant lay upon a cushion of white satin richly embroidered with coloured silks, and trimmed like the sheet; and was itself a mass of gold brocade and diamonds. But the young mother principally attracted my attention.

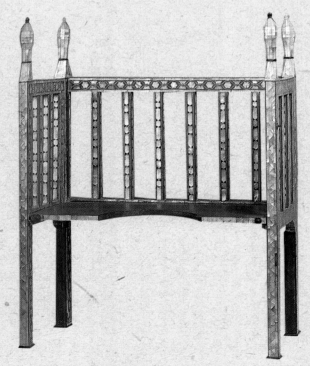

Birthing chair,
18–19th century

73

"Her dark hair was braided in twenty or thirty small plaits, that fell far below her waist... Her throat was encircled by several rows of immense pearls, whence depended a diamond star, resting upon her bosom; her chemisette was delicately edged with a gold beading, and met at the bottom of her bust, where her vest was confined by a costly shawl. Her head-dress, of blue gauze worked with silver, was studded with diamond sprays, and ornamented with a fringe of large gold coins, which fell upon her shoulders, and almost concealed her brilliant ear-rings. Her satin antery was of the most lively colours, and her salva were of pale pink silk, sprinkled with silver spots. A glass of white lilies rested against her pillow, and a fan of peacocks' feathers, and a painted handkerchief, lay beside her."[70]

The new mother remained *lohusa* for forty days to permit her internal organs to recuperate. On the fortieth day after birth, an elaborate celebration was held at the public bath. The mother and child were bathed amidst special ceremonies. The mother's body was plastered with a healing ointment "composed of honey and various aromatic condiments, held to possess strengthening and recuperating properties."[71] After about an hour, the ointment would be washed off, and the mother, dressed in a robe with gold or silver embroidered edges, would return to her guests in the cool room. After the new mother kissed the hands of her elders, entertainment was made and refreshments were served throughout the rest of the day.

There were many other special occasions that enlivened harem life, like celebrations of a child's first tooth, a child's first complete recitation of the Holy Qur'an, the first day of school, a boy's circumcision, a girl's first veiling, the sending off and return of a soldier and the return of a *hacı* from the holy pilgrimage to Mecca. Frequent visits were also a common event in the harem.

Visits among relatives often lasted for extended periods of time. Many Ottoman women held a *kabul günü* once a month at which time they would officially receive visitors. At the same time, drop-in visitors were always welcomed, as were female vendors. In addition, there were *masalcı* women or storytellers who were invited to entertain in the harem, especially on long, cold winter evenings. Preparation of trousseaus also occupied a great deal of time for women, their daughters and other female relatives. Most Ottoman women were highly accomplished in the art of embroidery, and they beautified all articles of clothing, bedding, towels, covers, and so forth.

Cradle. Topkapı Palace Museum

Melling, *Hatice Sultan Palace*, interior. 19th century.

Religious Holidays

Other significant times for celebration in the harem were Islamic religious holidays. In Islam there are a number of *kandils* or religious celebrations commemorating particular events like the birth of the Prophet Muhammad (peace be upon him), the night of his conception, his ascension to the heavens and others. There are two major religious celebrations, one of which is the four-day Eid ul-Adha, a commemoration of Prophet Abraham's (peace be upon him) sacrifice of a ram in lieu of his son Ishmael. During this holy celebration Muslims who can afford it sacrifice a sheep or a group sacrifices a cow or camel. One third of the meat is distributed to the poor and one third to relatives, and one third can be kept for the immediate family. In addition to making a sacrifice, visits are made to friends and relatives, gifts are given to family members and children, and alms are given to the poor.

Wall decoration. Fruit Room, Topkapı Palace

The other major religious holiday is Eid ul-Fitr, which is celebrated after one month of fasting and worship during the month of Ramadan in lunar calendar. Emine Fuat Tugay gave the following details about Ramadan in her childhood:

"During the month of Ramadan ... gates and house doors would be opened to the public. An imam *and a* muezzin *were engaged for the whole month at our house, and the latter would chant the call to evening prayer from the top of the stairs leading into the garden. Prayer-rugs facing south-east towards Mecca had been spread in the main hall for the men, and the drawing-rooms were similarly prepared for the women. As soon as a cannon boomed, announcing that the sun had set, the fast was broken with olives and bread, prior to the short evening prayer. The household, with its resident guests and any strangers who had come in, then sat down at different tables to 'iftar,' as the first meal after the fast is called. The men were all served in the* selamlik, *whether they were known to my father or not. He dined separately with his guests, but the food was the same for all.*

77

"Strange women did not often come to iftar, nevertheless a table was always ready for the 'Allah misafiri,' the guests of God. Special dishes were served at iftar. Black and green olives, several kinds of sliced cheese, a variety of jams, very thin slices of a sausage made from mutton, and the dried meat of mutton or turkey, the two last-named being the only foods flavored with garlic which were ever eaten in the konaks, had been placed, each one separately, in tiny dishes before each plate. Goblets containing sherbet always stood beside the glasses for water. The meal invariably began with soup, followed by eggs cooked either with cheese or meat, sausage, or dried meat, and usually ended after a large number of courses with the serving of 'güllaç,' a sweet made from thin wafers of starch. Two hours after sunset, the muezzin again chanted his call to the last prayer of the day, the 'Yatsi Namaz.' During Ramadan only, another prayer, the 'Teravih Namaz,' immediately follows the yatsi, both together lasting over an hour. My father, with his sons and household and those of his guests who wished to participate, never missed any of these prayers. I used to pray with the other women in the drawing-room, where screens placed in front of the wide-open double doors enabled them to hear the recitations without being seen. Those who fast are permitted two meals only, the sahur, an hour before sunrise, and the iftar on sunset. During the interval nothing may pass down the throat, even smoking being prohibited, since smoke can be swallowed."[72]

After the teravih prayer, people usually stayed up all night until the sahur meal before sunrise. Some of the time might be spent in religious devotion, but there were amusements in the harem as well. One of the most popular persons during Ramadan evenings was the storyteller woman, who would be hired to enchant her listeners with imaginary tales. Also there were public festivities special to the month of Ramadan. The minarets were all lit up and there were banners hung between the minarets with illuminated designs and good wishes. Occasional fireworks would further light up the skies. The public squares would be filled with people taking part in the Ramadan festivities.

The twenty-seventh night of Ramadan is an especially holy time called Kadir Gecesi, or the Night of Power. Worship on this night has power equal to one thousand months of worship. The mosques would overflow with people, some of whom would spend the whole night in worship. Women, who did not regularly attend prayer services at the mosques, would sometimes participate in the mosque services as well. Others spent Kadir Gecesi in worship in the privacy of the harem.

Preparations for the three-day celebration that begins after the end of the month of Ramadan would begin a week earlier. The houses were thoroughly cleaned from top to bottom and special dishes, particularly sweets like baklava, would be prepared in anticipation of guests to come. A new suit of clothing would be either bought or sewn for everyone. Lucy Garnett described the Ramadan holiday activities:

"The conclusion of Ramadan is celebrated by the three days' festival of 'Bairam,' also called by names signifying respectively the 'Breaking of the Fast' and the 'Feast of Alms,' during which no work of any kind is done. On the first day of Bairam, every well-to-do person makes a present to his children, his slaves, and his subordinates, besides giving liberally to the poor. In the mornings the streets are thronged with people in holiday costume, who go from house to house paying complimentary visits to friends and official superiors; and after attending the 'midday namaz' in the mosques, the whole Moslem population abandons itself to decorous amusement."[73]

Outings

In addition to paying visits to friends, relatives and neighbors, attending special occasions like weddings and births in other harems, and celebrating religious holidays by means of short excursions and visits on Eid, it was the custom of most Ottoman women to go out to a public bath once a week. This was an event at which women not only bathed and groomed their bodies, but it was a day of socializing with many other women as well. The women often took their small children with them and were accompanied by a party of slaves (according to their means), who carried with them in bundles all items necessary for bathing such as towels, basins, soap and combs. The servants also brought clothing to be put on after the bath and plenty of food and refreshments as the bath was an all-day affair.

Inside the bath women wore raised wooden clogs which were usually decorated with silver or inlaid mother-of-pearl and a thin linen wrap. There were several different rooms, the first one being the cooling room, which is described as follows by Julia Pardoe:

"Having passed through a small entrance-court, we entered an extensive hall, paved with white marble, and surrounded by a double tier of projecting galleries, supported by pillars; the lower range being raised about three feet from the floor. These galleries were covered with rich carpets, or mattresses, overlaid with chintz or crimson shag, and crowded with cushions; the spaces

between the pillars were slightly partitioned off to the height of a few inches; and, when we enter, the whole of the boxes, if I may so call them, were occupied, save the one which had been reserved for us.

"In the centre of the hall, a large and handsome fountain of white marble, pouring its waters into four ample scallop-shells, whence they fell again into a large basin with the prettiest and most soothing sound imaginable, was surrounded by four sofas of the same material, on one of which a young and lovely woman lay pillowed on several costly shawls, nursing her infant.

The boxes presented the oddest appearance in the world—some of the ladies had returned from the bathing-hall, and were reclining luxuriously upon their sofas, rolled from head to foot in fine white linen, in many instances embroidered and fringed with gold, with their fine hair falling about their shoulders, which their slaves, not quite so closely covered as their mistresses, were drying, combing, perfuming, and plaiting, with the greatest care. Others were preparing for the bath, and laying aside their dresses ... while the latest comers were removing their 'yashmacs' and cloaks, and exchanging greetings with their acquaintance."[74]

The second hall of the bath was called the "cooling room," where women remained for some time lying round and relaxing after coming out of the "hot room," or main bathing area. There were a number of fountains (Pardoe counted eight) in the

Tristam (Tristram), *Excursion on the Golden Horn*, 1888

main hall for bathing, available to those who could not afford a private bathing booth. Two pipes of water, one hot water and the other cold water, ran into a marble basin from which water was poured on to the bather either by her personal slave or by bath attendants. Women usually spent a couple of hours in the hot room, where every kind of hygienic and beautifying process was completed, similar to today's spas. Depilatory paste and perfumed soaps were used on the body, and natural dyes and henna were used on the hair and nails.

After the bath was complete and the women had reclined for some time in the cooling room, they returned to the first room, a kind of lounge, where there was a very festive atmosphere. There they dined, listened to music, were entertained by dancing girls and chatted with other women. In addition to the foods that had been brought from home, there was fruit, pudding, sherbet and lemonade available for sale. After catching up on all the recent news, the women would return to the privacy of their own harems.

Another favorite outing of Ottoman women was the picnic. During fair weather women would flock to the meadows of Kağıthane and the Göksu valley or to different spots on the shores of the Bosphorus. They frequently traveled by means of *araba*s or covered carts drawn by oxen. Men would usually ride on horses or mules. If crossing over the Bosphorus Straits, they traveled by *caiques*. After arriving at the picnic area, men sat separately from the women and children. Servants would prepare the picnic spreads and, in addition to plentiful food brought from home, there were many sellers of puddings, sherbets and various sweets. Both Ottoman women and men had a strong love for nature, and picnics provided them with just the right setting to indulge this pleasure.

Julia Pardoe painted in words the enchanting atmosphere of Ottoman picnics:

"The Valley of Guiuk-Suy [Göksu], thronged as I have attempted to describe it, presents a scene essentially Oriental in its character. The crimson-covered carriages moving along beneath the trees, the white-veiled groups scattered over the fresh turf, the constant motion of the attendant slaves, the quaintly-dressed venders of 'mohalibe' and 'sekel' (or sweetmeats) moving rapidly from point to point with their plateaux upon their heads, furnished with a raised shelf, on which the crystal or china plates destined to serve for the one, and the pink and yellow glories of the other, are temptingly displayed; the 'yahourt' [yogurt] merchant, with his yoke upon his shoulder, and his swinging trays covered with little brown clay basins, showing forth the creamy whiteness of his merchandise; the

Liotard, *Turkish Woman with her Slave,* 18th century ▶

Bowl. Silver, 19th century

82

vagrant exhibitors of dancing bears and grinning monkeys; the sunburnt Greek, with his large, flapping hat of Leghorn straw, and Frank costume, hurrying along from group to group with his pails of ice; and recommending his delicate and perishable luxury in as many languages as he is likely to earn piastres; the never-failing water-carrier, with his large turban, his graceful jar of red earth, and his crystal goblet; the negroes of the higher harems, laden with carpets, chibouks, and refreshments for their mistresses; the fruit-vendors, with their ruddy peaches, their clusters of purple grapes from Smyrna, their pyramidically-piled filberts, and their rich plums, clothed in bloom, and gathered with their fresh leaves about them; the melon-merchants sitting among their unheaped riches; the 'pasteks' with their emerald-coloured rinds, and the musk-melons, looking like golden balls, and scenting the breeze as it sweeps over them; the variety of costume exhibited by the natives, always most striking on the Asiatic shore; the ringing rattle of the tambourine, and the sharp wiry sound of the Turkish Zebec, accompanied by the shrill voices of half a dozen Greeks, seated in a semicircle in front of a beauty-laden araba—all combine to complete a picture so perfect of its kind, that, were an European to be transported to Guiuk-Suy, without any intermediate preparation, he would believe himself to be under the spell of an Enchanter, and beholding the realization of what he had hitherto considered as the mere extravagance of some Eastern story-teller."[75]

Yet another source of pleasure for Ottoman women were the illuminations commemorating important events such as the Prophet Muhammad's birthday or celebrations regarding the royal family. The parks, gardens and facades of houses along the Bosphorus shore would be illuminated with thousands of little lamps made into magnificent designs in honor of the special occasion. The gardens were open to the public for viewing the different illuminations, and many would go by boat up and down the Bosphorus. Emine Fuat Tugay gave a first-hand description of the illuminations for the Sultan's birthday that she witnessed as a child:

"We children first admired our garden from the windows, and then soon steamed off in my father's launch to look at the illuminations along the shore of the Bosphorus. The whole family, with a few intimate friends, left the landing-stage at Moda and then sat watching the city unfolding its galaxy of lights, and with these the long glittering facade of the Dolma Bahçe Palace, all reflected in the water. A row of palaces, many of them now no more in

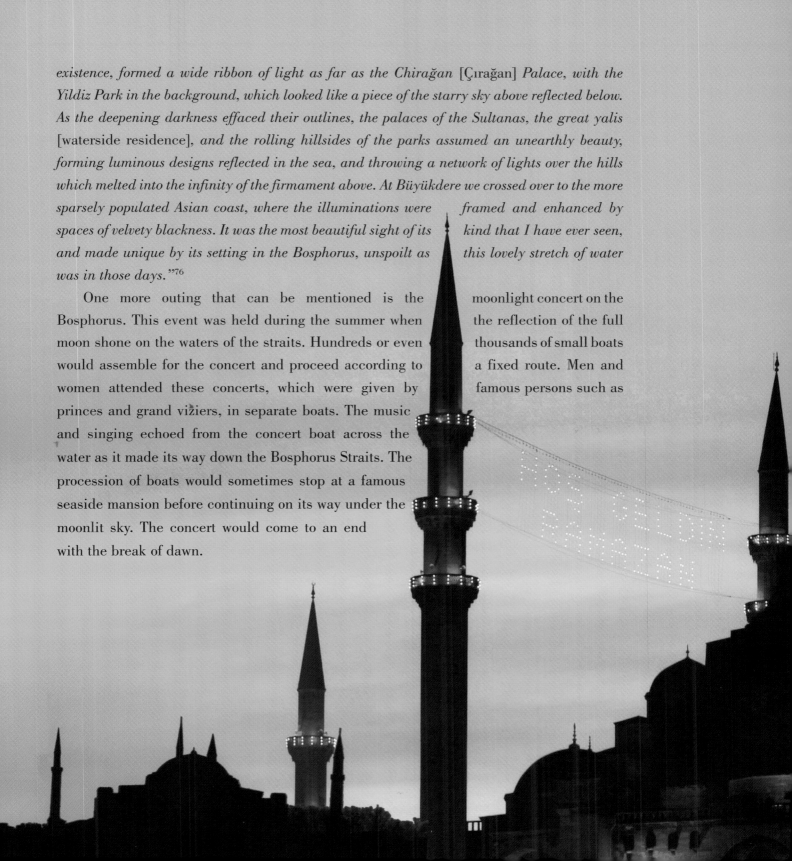

existence, formed a wide ribbon of light as far as the Chiragan [Çırağan] Palace, with the Yildiz Park in the background, which looked like a piece of the starry sky above reflected below. As the deepening darkness effaced their outlines, the palaces of the Sultanas, the great yalis [waterside residence], and the rolling hillsides of the parks assumed an unearthly beauty, forming luminous designs reflected in the sea, and throwing a network of lights over the hills which melted into the infinity of the firmament above. At Büyükdere we crossed over to the more sparsely populated Asian coast, where the illuminations were framed and enhanced by *spaces of velvety blackness. It was the most beautiful sight of its* kind that I have ever seen, *and made unique by its setting in the Bosphorus, unspoilt as* this lovely stretch of water *was in those days."76*

One more outing that can be mentioned is the moonlight concert on the Bosphorus. This event was held during the summer when the reflection of the full moon shone on the waters of the straits. Hundreds or even thousands of small boats would assemble for the concert and proceed according to a fixed route. Men and women attended these concerts, which were given by famous persons such as princes and grand viziers, in separate boats. The music and singing echoed from the concert boat across the water as it made its way down the Bosphorus Straits. The procession of boats would sometimes stop at a famous seaside mansion before continuing on its way under the moonlit sky. The concert would come to an end with the break of dawn.

Rogier, *Washing Hands in the Harem*, 1848

III

Ottoman Women as Slaves in the Harem

Were I a man, and condemned to an existence of servitude, I would unhesitatingly choose that of slavery in a Turkish family; for if ever the "bitter drought" can indeed be rendered palatable, it is there. The slave of the Osmanli is the child of his adoption; he purchases with his gold a being to cherish, to protect, and to support; and in almost every case he secures to himself what all his gold could not command—a devoted and loving heart, ready to sacrifice its every hope and impulse in his service. One forgets that the smiling menial who hands you your coffee, or pours the rose-water from an urn of silver, has been purchased at a price, and you must look with admiration on the relative positions of the servant and his lord—the one so eager and so earnest in his services—the other so gentle and so unexacting in his commands.[77]

Julia Pardoe, 1836

Female Slaves in the Household Harem

It was the consensus among European travelers that slavery under the Ottomans was similar to slavery in the West in name only. There were significant reasons for this. To begin with, slavery under the Ottomans was not a system of forced hard labor on agricultural plantations as it was in the West. Male Ottoman slaves were basically military or domestic slaves, and females were mainly domestic slaves. African women usually worked as cooks and did menial tasks, while white female slaves performed more specialized tasks like making and serving coffee or spreading and attending the dinner trays or acting as a nursemaid. European women who visited Ottoman harems reported that all of the slave women had an astonishingly abundant amount of leisure time and freedom of speech and action inside the harem. Moreover, they considered the slave girl's lot in Turkey to be "preferable to that of the domestic servant in the West."[78]

Secondly, slavery was temporary. White women were obliged to serve as slaves for nine years, but black women, coming from Africa, only had to serve for seven years because their constitutions were less well suited to a colder climate. When a woman was freed from slavery, she would receive a legally valid certificate of emancipation. She could request either to remain for the rest of her life with her former master's family, in which case she would be well taken care of, or request to be married. When married, she received jewelry, a trousseau, furniture and, more than likely, a house of her own. The freed slave always received a pension for life from her former master. In addition, she kept strong ties with her former family and could depend on them in time of need. Many former slave women, particularly those trained in the harems of the elite, married men of high position. As a result, slavery can be seen as a vehicle of upper mobility in Ottoman society. In fact, according to Adolphus Slade, "slavery was to oriental women what India had been to English men: a social ladder."[79]

Thirdly, there was no social stigma to slavery in Ottoman society. After the fourteenth century, when Ottoman sultans began to take slave concubines as mates rather than marrying free women as wives, most of the sultans themselves were the sons of former slave women. The *valide sultan* or queen mother, who had the most elevated position of any woman in the Ottoman Empire, was most likely a former slave. The military and administrative elite were drawn heavily from former male slaves who had been educated and trained in the schools of the Imperial Palace. Their wives were often former slave women who had been trained in refined Ottoman etiquette and accomplishments within the imperial harem or other great Ottoman harems. Consequently, slavery was not a badge of disdain for slave women; on the contrary, a woman's having been raised and groomed as a slave girl in one of the great harems was an important point of attraction for ambitious potential husbands, who would want to forge a strong connection to a family from the elite ruling strata of society.

As a result of these social circumstances, many young girls, themselves, volunteered to become slaves or their families sold them into slavery believing

PAGE 87: Ewer and basin, 18th century

Liotard, *Portrait of Maria Adelaide of France in Turkish Costume*, 1753

89

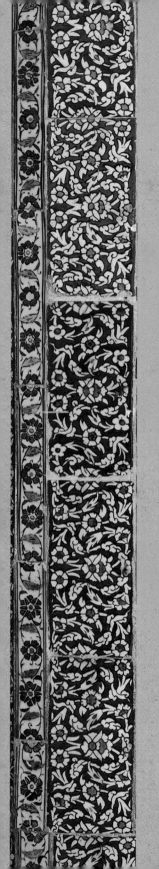

they would have a better future as slaves. This was particularly true for Circassian girls, who along with Georgian girls, made up most of the white female slave population beginning in the eighteenth century. According to Pardoe, almost all girls and boys in Circassia insisted upon being taken to Istanbul, "where the road to honour and advancement is open to everyone."[80] Due to the feudal social system existent in the Caucasus at that time, which consisted of princes, nobles and slaves, children of slave families were customarily sold for the profit of their owners. Others might be captured during tribal raids and sold to slave dealers for profit as well. Regardless of whether slavery was voluntary or forced, it was definitely seen as a transitory phase leading to social advancement by both the children and their parents. An anecdote related by Fanny Davis shows how adamant Circassian mothers were to have their daughters become slaves in Ottoman harems:

"In 1856–1857 Lady Blunt's brother and brother-in-law made a trip into the Caucasus with the aim of persuading parents to stop selling their children. They equipped themselves with presents of lokum *[Turkish delight] and finery, only to have their gifts refused. Mothers were indignant at what they felt were attempts to keep their daughters from getting to Istanbul and advancing themselves. Each had a vision of her daughter entering the* saray *[palace] and becoming valide sultan."*[81]

Of course, the benign treatment of slaves in Ottoman harems was another important factor in the attraction of slavery under the Ottomans for the girls and their families as well. Young slave girls were raised as a part of the family in the true sense of the word. Strong bonds were forged between the slaves and members of their foster family. They were often bought at a young age, such as six or seven, or sometimes even as infants, in which case they were provided with wet nurses. Upon entering her new home, the young slave girl was given a new poetical name like "Dilshad (heart's joy)" or "Dilruba" (captor of hearts) and assigned to one of the experienced slave women. She ate the same food as the family members did, and her clothing was similar in quality to theirs. The young slave girl was trained in the elaborate Ottoman etiquette and practiced it by waiting on the older slave women before directly serving family members. She was taught to speak and read Turkish, and she was also taught the basic beliefs and practices of Islam. In addition, she learned to sew and embroider. If she had musical talent, she would be taught how to play an instrument or to sing and dance, and if she had any other special talent, that would be cultivated as well. Some girls were bought as companions for the

Osman Hamdi, *Two Musician Girls*, 1880

young girls in the family, and they were given the same education as family members. Some learned to read Persian and Arabic and, in later centuries, English and French. Some slave girls were trained to be nursemaids for the children of the family. In general, they were taught all the accomplishments and manners that a free Ottoman girl would know. Commenting on the fate of the slave girl, Ferriman wrote, *"Slavery under the conditions above described can scarcely be called a misfortune. The ... child exchanges the hardships of barbarism for comfort, often for luxury and refinement; her duties are light... In short, she steps from savagery into civilization."*[82]

Once the slave girls had completed their term of servitude, they were married to Ottoman men. Sometimes they were freed before their term was completed because the emancipation of slaves is considered to be an act of great moral value in Islam. In either case, these women usually made very favorable marriages. Because of their beauty, charm and cultivation, they were highly sought after as brides. Many were married to the sons of the families they grew up in. Others were married to male members of the Ottoman ruling class, many of whom were also former slaves. Some men preferred to marry slaves or former slaves because the expense was considerably less than if they were to marry free Ottoman women of the ruling class. In fact, there were female slave traders, many of them former slaves themselves, who bought very young girls, raised and trained them until the girls were of marriageable age, and then sold them at lucrative prices. The duty of finding a husband for the slave girls fell to the mistress of the house, who fulfilled this obligation conscientiously because it was a point of honor for her to marry her slaves well. The slave's foster family also provided her trousseau, home furnishings and often a house as well. Emine Fuat Tugay mentions a freed slave who had been given two houses upon her marriage by Tugay's grandmother.[83] Leyla Saz describes a typical dowry of a nineteenth century slave woman as follows:

"Other than the small presents that she had received during her servitude, she then received some jewelry, earrings, a diamond ring, a watch in gold along with silver saucers and a coffee set. She also was given delicate little spoons made of rhinoceros horns, of ivory or even of tortoise shells, along with all the necessary furnishings for a household. The richness of the trousseau matched the wealth of the mistress and the rank which she herself had occupied as a slave in the household. There were many masters who even bought them a little house while marrying them off and even in our day there are many young ladies of fine circumstances who

would not be embarrassed at all to have a trousseau and furnishings of one of these kalfas *who had left a 'konak' with the blessings of their mistresses and masters."*[84]

The slave's ties to her foster family continued throughout her lifetime and even beyond in many cases, as the foster family often helped the children of their former slaves as well. In some cases, the slaves requested to remain in their foster family rather than marry, in which case they were taken care of for the rest of their lives. For example, the nurse of Leyla Saz's sister refused to leave the family and tore up with her own hands the certificate of freedom which they had tried to give her. She raised the sister's children and died in their house at the age of sixty.[85]

Slavery was strictly regulated in the Ottoman Empire by Islamic law. The slave girl's rights and her master's or mistress's responsibilities towards her were clearly defined. Once purchased, no slave girl could be turned out onto the streets. Her owner either had to sell her, free her, give her to someone else or provide for her himself. If a concubine bore her master a child, she gained the legal status of *ümm-ül veled* (mother of a child), and, as a consequence, she could not be sold or given away and she became free when her master died, if not freed beforehand. When the father acknowledged the child, as he almost always did, it was considered legitimate and free and would inherit the same as any child from a legal marriage. The mother was often married to her master or married to an outsider and provided with a dowry.[86] If slaves were unhappy, they could ask to be resold and they had the legal support of the law. If their owners refused, the slaves could run away. However, they could not obtain freedom by running away before their term of servitude was complete. If they ran away, they had to apply to a slave dealer, who would sell them to a new owner and inform their former master.

Many Europeans mentioned the indulgence shown to Ottoman slaves by their masters and mistresses. Tugay gives an example of indulgent treatment in regard to one of the female slaves of her grandfather, the Khedive of Egypt. The slave woman frequently complained of illness, upon which the palace physician, a *pasha* (general) would be called in. An older slave woman noticed that the younger woman was exaggerating her condition and that the doctor was holding her wrist longer than usual. When the young slave woman and doctor were questioned, they admitted a mutual attachment. They were subsequently married and the former slave woman was given five hundred *feddan*s of farmland in addition to the customary jewels and trousseau. They drove to her husband's house in the ex-slave woman's own carriage, another gift from her former master.[87]

There are two recorded instances in which slave girls even refused a sultan's attentions. The first incident was related by Julia Pardoe. She actually met the slave girl named Nazip, who refused an offer to become a part of Sultan Mahmud II's harem. She described the incident as follows:

"Asme Sultane (sister of Mahmud II) is celebrated throughout the capital for the beauty of her slaves; and his Sublime Highness has thrice demanded Nazip Hanoum, but has been thrice refused; an occurrence so unprecedented in the East, that he has finished by persuading himself that he is actually attached to the lively girl who has dared to play the part of a modern Roxalana, and defy his power.

"His first rejection was treated by the Sultan as the wayward whim of a spoiled beauty, and even he condescended to expostulate with Nazip Hanoum; but his advice had no more effect upon her than his preference; and, for the first time in his life, the 'Brother of the Sun' and 'Emperor of the Earth' found himself slighted by a mere girl."[88]

The second incident was related by Ayşe Sultan, the daughter of Sultan Abdülhamid II. According to Ayşe Sultan, her father was very much taken by a beautiful Georgian slave girl in the palace. He paid the lovely slave many compliments and showered attention upon her, but the Georgian beauty refused the Sultan's entreaties for five years. When she went to pay her respects to Sultan Abdülhamid II on one of the religious holy days, he first told her how beautiful she looked and then asked if she was persisting in her stubbornness. She replied, "My Master, as long as I am alive I will be ready to sacrifice my life for

Sultan
Abdülhamid II
(1842–1918)

you. I will not desert you. But if you grant me the whole world, I will not become your concubine... because the man who will become my husband must have only one wife; that is, I wish him to belong only to me. Otherwise, I will not marry anyone." Unsuccessful in fulfilling his desire for the Georgian beauty, the Sultan acquiesced to her refusal. He bought and furnished a house for her and married the beautiful slave girl to a devout man forty-five years of age. However, Sultan Abdülhamid II called the groom to his presence on the wedding night and kept him at the palace until dawn. The Sultan repeated this procedure for five consecutive nights after the wedding.[89]

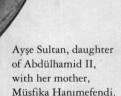

Ayşe Sultan, daughter of Abdülhamid II, with her mother, Müşfika Hanımefendi.

Female Slaves in the Imperial Harem

It appears that in Ottoman household harems female slaves were used primarily as servants to the family, although some were used as concubines as well. In the imperial harem, however, the role of concubines was much greater. By the end of the fourteenth century concubinage played a major role in royal reproduction.[90] Previous Muslim dynasties like the Abbasids had practiced royal concubinage, but the Ottomans gave greater importance to it as a dynastic policy of reproduction. There were a number of benefits to the Ottoman dynasty deriving from royal concubinage. First of all, it was seen as preferable to have female consorts whose allegiance was exclusive to the sultan rather than having wives from a pool of hereditary nobility who might challenge the sultan's power. This was a policy pursued in regard to the military and administrative elite as well, many of whom were chosen from a pool of highly trained, loyal, male slaves or former slaves. Secondly, there was the practice of a royal consort usually having only one son because, as the mentor as well as mother of a prince, she needed to devote herself completely to his training and protection. It would not have been legally possible to force a free Muslim wife to restrict herself to one son. Thirdly, with the high rate of infant mortality, disease and death on the battlefield, it was more logical not to rely on only one woman's ability to produce sons for the continuation of the dynasty.[91]

Although concubines played a very important role in the Ottoman dynasty's policy of reproduction, it would be erroneous to think that most slave girls in the imperial harem were concubines of the sultan. In fact, only approximately ten percent[92] of female slaves were concubines. This figure included concubines of the Ottoman princes, as well, who also lived in the royal palace. Only very select slave women at the top of the palace training system, who excelled in intelligence, character and accomplishments, as well as beauty, were eligible as concubine candidates. These women were often trained by the sultan's mother, herself, or were gifts from other royal family members or highly placed officials. Other slave women in the imperial harem could aspire to rise in the administrative ranks to a permanent career within the harem institution or hope to be manumitted and married to a husband in the Ottoman military or administrative elite. After such a marriage, they would head their own harem which might be quite large, depending upon their husband's status.

In addition to being a residence for the royal family, the imperial harem was, more than anything else, a training institution for women who would become a part of the royal family, for female attendants to the royal family, for servants in the daily administration of the imperial harem and for women who would become wives of the Ottoman elite. There was a very strict and elaborate etiquette observed in the imperial harem at all times. All activities were conducted in accordance with it. Even the sultan was bound by it; for example, he had to receive his consorts in a strict order so that none of the women's turn was missed unless she, herself, was indisposed. A rule of silence was strictly enforced near the sultan's private premises, prompting some Westerners to compare the imperial harem with a monastery. Commenting on the solemnity of the imperial harem in 1695, François Petis de la Croix stated:

"I can, my dear brother, more easily than any other, satisfy your curiosity about the Seraglio of the Ottoman Emperors, for, having been confined in it more than twenty years, I have had the time to observe its beauties, its way of life, its discipline. If one believed the many fantastical descriptions of various foreign travelers, some of which have been translated into our language, it would be difficult not to imagine that this Palace was an enchanted

Lewis, *In the Bey's Garden*, 1865

Jeweled cup, 16th century

place....But its principal beauty lies in the order which one observes within it and the education of those who are destined for the service of the powerful who inhabit it."[93]

There were many similarities between the organization of the imperial harem and the third courtyard, the home of the male slaves, eunuchs and pages, who were in the personal service of the sultan. There were similarities both in their rank and in the institutional career paths of the female and male slaves-in-training. The daily stipends the male and female slaves received were also similar. For example, the average stipend of the female slaves in the New Palace in 1652, except for the highest ranking group, was 8.7 aspers per day. The average daily stipend of the male pages in training was 8.5 aspers in 1664.[94]

When new slave girls were brought to the imperial palace, they were thoroughly trained by the older slave women or by special teachers brought to the palace. The girls were taught the basic tenets and practices of Islam and they learned to read the Qur'an, as well. They were also instructed in the Turkish language. They all learned to speak and read Turkish, and some slave girls were taught to write as well. In particular, all the wives of the sultans could write and they usually had a bookcase in their room.[95] The novices were taught to sew and embroider also, and when they were not busy with other work, the women in the palace spent much time embroidering. Those musically inclined were trained to sing, play musical instruments and dance. The girls were also instructed in the ceremonies, customs and refined etiquette of the royal residence. In general, an air of discipline and industriousness pervaded the halls of the imperial harem. In a sense, it could be called the royal finishing school because it was there that young slave girls learned the arts and skills necessary for the roles they were destined to play as a part of the royal family and the Ottoman elite.

Painter unknown, *Enjoying Coffee*, 18th century

Hilair, *Ladies of the harem taking a walk*, 1797

IV

Ottoman Women in the Imperial Harem

From the time of Süleyman, the inner palace was increasingly the central arena of government. Its inhabitants—the sultan's favorites and eunuchs, his mother and his 'hasekis,' and the harem's officers and black eunuch guards— acquired both formal and informal influence over the sultan's decisions. Far from being isolated from public events, the high-ranking women of the harem lived at the very heart of political life.[96]

Leslie Pierce, author of *The Imperial Harem*

Wall recess. Sultan
Ahmed I Privy
Chamber

A strict hierarchy of rank and power existed among the women living in the imperial harem. The sultan's mother, the *valide sultan*, stood alone at the top of the hierarchical pyramid. Her authority was absolute in the harem, and she was respected and deferred to by all those living in the imperial palace and the general populace as well. The royal concubines stood next in the hierarchy, but they were not all on an equal footing. There was a hierarchy of rank among them according to the order in which they had been favored by the sultan. The first chosen was called *baş kadın efendi* or chief lady. The others were designated as *kadın efendi II, III and IV*. Although they usually had slave status and were therefore not legal wives, they had the social status of royal wife and their number was usually limited to four, the maximum number of wives legally permitted in Islam. Following the *kadın*s were other consorts of the sultan called *ikbal*s, who also were numbered according to the order in which they were elevated to that position. Whenever one of the women died, all of the subsequent concubines moved up in status. Next in rank came the daughters of the sultan, who were also given the title of sultan, followed by the *daye hatun*, the sultan's wet nurse, and the *kethüda hatun*, the senior administrative official in the imperial harem. The household staff followed and, at the base of the hierarchy, came the slave women who performed menial tasks. Approximately ninety percent of the slave women in the imperial harem worked as servants only and had no intimate relationship with the sultan.[97]

Valide Sultan

Upon a new sultan's ascension to the throne, he would call his mother from the Old Palace, where most retired royal consorts lived. She would proceed in state to the Topkapı Palace, where her son was awaiting her arrival. All echelons of the Ottoman military and administrative elite were present at this event, which indicates the high status of the *valide sultan*. The great respect in which the queen mother was held by her son is obvious in the following passage, where the sultan meets her on foot at the palace and bows before her, an honor that no one else in the Ottoman Empire received. This passage describes the *valide sultan* procession of Sultan Selim III's mother, Mihrişah, which included between eighty to one hundred carriages:

Twin Pavilions, Topkapı Palace

"The Divan heralds with plaited turbans fell in front; then walked, also with plaited turbans, those who were connected with the Holy Cities, either as appointees or as administrators; after them came the 'valide's kethüda,' Mahmut Bey, with his [turban], and wide-sleeved sable fur and a sceptor in his hand; after him 'baltacıs' [halberdiers] on both sides, and then the Ağa [of the House of Felicity] with plaited turban, and after him passed the 'valide sultan,' in a six-horse carriage with drawn curtains, and behind her another official scattering bright money on both sides. Behind the 'valide's' carriage were the slaves and 'sultanas' being transported to the New Palace.

"The 'valide's' procession entered through the Bab-ı Hümayun [Imperial Gate], *and when it came to the imperial bakery Sultan Selim came to meet his mother and gave her the oriental salute [temenna] three times and kissed his mother's hand through the window of the carriage, which was open on the right side, and fell in front of her and took her to the imperial harem."*[98]

The mother of the sultan was much more than just a mother to her son. She was also his teacher, his mentor, his confidant, his strongest ally, his protector and, if need be, his regent. Thus, it was only natural for a prince to show strong devotion to his mother when he became sultan. There are many examples of *valide sultans* who exerted strong influence on their sons. Gülbahar Sultan (mother of Beyazid II), Hafsa Sultan (mother of Süleyman), Nurbanu Sultan (mother of Murad III), Safiye Sultan (mother of Mehmed III), Gülnuş Sultan (mother of Mustafa II and Ahmed III), Mihrişah Sultan (mother of Selim III), and Bezm-i Alem Sultan (mother of Abdülmecid) are all queen mothers who exerted their wills in affairs of state.[99] One of the most powerful *valide sultans* was Kösem Sultan (d. 1651), mother of Murad IV, who became sultan at the young age of twelve, and Ibrahim, who was emotionally disturbed. Kösem Sultan was the daughter of a Greek priest. After being orphaned, she fell into the hands of the Ottoman governor general of Bosnia who presented her to the imperial palace. For decades, the control of Ottoman affairs lay in the hands of this queen mother, who has been criticized by some for her heavy-handed tactics. Her rule came to a violent end when she refused to turn over the power to her daughter-in-law Turhan Sultan upon the ascension of Kösem Sultan's grandson and Turhan Sultan's son, the seven-year-old Mehmed IV. Kösem Sultan intended to have Mehmed dethroned in place of another young grandson with a more compatible mother, but Turhan Sultan learned of her plot and informed the head black eunuch, who murdered Kösem Sultan in a pre-emptive strike.[100]

The natural closeness of the mother-son relationship in the Ottoman dynasty continued until death parted them. The depth of this bond is beautifully exemplified by the following account of the funeral ceremony of Nurbanu Sultan, mother of Sultan Murad III:

"Contrary to the custom whereby the sultan remained in the palace during a funeral, Murad accompanied his mother's coffin on foot, weeping as he walked, to the mosque of Mehmed the Conqueror, where funeral prayers were said. The choice of the Conqueror's mosque, the most distant of the sultanic mosques from the imperial palace, ensured both a maximum number of bystanders' prayers for Nurbanu's soul and maximum appreciation by the capital's residents of this display of royal piety and respect for the valide sultan. *According to the historian Selanki, the 'whole world' crowded into the mosque for the funeral prayers. For forty days, high-ranking statesmen and religious officials were required to pay their respects at the* valide sultan's *tomb, while the Qur'an was read continuously."*[101]

Head of the Imperial Harem

All of the women residents in the imperial harem were paid a daily stipend from the imperial treasury. The *valide sultan*'s stipend was the highest in the Ottoman Empire, frequently several times greater than the sultan's, thus reflecting her extraordinary status.[102] Her living quarters were magnificent as well. The largest of any in the harem except for the sultan's, the *valide sultan*'s suite of rooms included a sitting room, a dining room, a bedroom, a bath, a kitchen and a pantry. The rooms of higher ranking harem women, especially the queen mother, were elegantly decorated with costly furnishings often containing valuable jewels and the most luxurious material available. The floors were covered with Egyptian rush mats in the summer and Persian carpets in the winter. There were crystal chandeliers hanging from the ceilings and gold and silver candle holders on the walls. Cushions covered with costly material rested on the divans placed against the walls. Velvet curtains in striking colors hung at the windows and doors. There were bowls made from crystal, gold and silver that had come from all over the world. Beautiful ceramic vases containing flowers were placed throughout the rooms and halls. Doors, bookcases and shelves were hand-carved in intricate designs and often ornamented with mother-of-pearl.[103] Since Topkapı Palace, Dolmabahçe Palace and Çırağan Palace were

all located on the Bosphorus Straits, many of the rooms had beautiful sea views. Situated between the apartments of the sultan and princes, on one side, and the slave women, on the other, the *valide sultan*'s suite enabled her to watch over both the family wing and the service wing.

All of the activities in the harem were under the command of the *valide sultan*. She had a large staff to assist her in the administrative work, and she ran the harem by means of the *kethüda usta* (head stewardess) and her assistant the *haznedâr usta*. The *valide sultan* assumed the lead female role at all royal ceremonies and celebrations, and she usually participated in the public Friday prayers. She also planned the seasonal moves of the harem from one palace to another and supervised other harem outings. Her outside business and property were overseen by a male steward, who received a fur coat and a dagger from the queen mother signifying the honor of the position he held. All residents of the harem greatly respected the *valide sultan* and none dared to cross her.

Royal Ottoman Matriarch

The duties of the queen mother were not limited to overseeing the imperial harem. At the same time she was the matriarch of the Ottoman dynasty, and she represented the royal family in public functions and ceremonies such as royal weddings and circumcisions. She was also the paramount female figure in palace events like royal births, the annual visit to

Loos, *Topkapı Palace*, 1710

the holy relics, religious celebrations, and so on. For example, it was custom for the imperial family to visit the holy mantle of the Prophet Muhammad in Topkapı Palace every year on the fifteenth of the month of Ramadan. When the doors of the room containing the Prophet's mantle were opened, the *valide sultan* would head the line of royal women as they filed past the holy relic. Amidst the scent of burning incense and the recitation of the Holy Qur'an, each woman would touch the mantle to her face and then salute the sultan before leaving. As a gift from the sultan, she would receive a handkerchief embroidered with a verse of poetry or a verse from the Qur'an which had been rubbed against the holy relic.[104]

Pasini, *A Corner of the Harem*, 1877

Another example of the queen mother's role as matriarch of the royal Ottoman family is the attendance of Valide Sultan Nurbanu at the circumcision of the son of Sultan Murad III, Mehmed. Taking place in 1582, the royal ceremonies and celebration continued for thirty-eight days. In order for the royal women to be able to observe events while still being concealed from the public eye, stations for viewing the spectacle were set up at a palace in the Hippodrome, where the festivities took place. On the day of the circumcision, the knife used on her grandson was presented to the *Valide Sultan*, who in turn bestowed three thousand gold coins, among other valuable gifts, upon the surgeon who performed the circumcision.[105]

The powerful position of *valide sultan* in her role as royal matriarch is obvious in the size and splendor of Valide Sultan Gülnuş's retinue as she re-entered Istanbul after having traveled to a royal palace in Edirne, a former Ottoman capital, in 1668. The details were described by a French jewel merchant who witnessed the three-hour long imperial procession:

"First to enter the city were two hundred mounted men of the Silahdar's [sword bearer] *retinue, followed by the retinue of the lieutenant grand vezir. Behind them rode four hundred men of the imperial cavalry, each wearing plaited armor and a short robe of taffeta and carrying a quiver covered in green velvet embroidered with gold wire and a bow in a matching case; their horses' trappings were of rich materials of yellow, red, or purple, worked with silver thread. Behind them rode their leader, with a helmet plume three feet high, followed by six attendants. Next marched a group of Janissaries and their commander, who wearing bells on their clothing and caps with donkey ears on their heads, carried silver staffs. Then came the lieutenant grand vezir, who was proceeded by one hundred guards, each carrying a spear with a banner attached, and three hundred fancily clad heralds. The vezir's party was followed by five to six hundred imperial gardeners. Next came representatives of the religious institution; two hundred judges in plain dress, wearing black boots of Morrocan leather and huge turbans, marched in strict discipline (in contrast to the disorganization of several of the groups). They were followed by sixty descendants of the Prophet, each wearing a turban of green, the color of the Prophet, and two officials dressed in white representing the* müfti.

At the end of the procession, leading the valide sultan's *retinue, was the* Silahdar *himself, riding a horse whose harness was of gold studded with pearls. He was followed by fifty riderless horses with sumptuous trappings, each led by a groom. Escorting the carriages of the women was a group of colorfully dressed black eunuchs. Turhan Sultan's carriage was drawn by six horses and surrounded by six guards who carried spears with red horse tails, symbols of sovereign power. The second carriage, presumably carrying the* haseki [the sultan's consort] *sultan Gülnuş, was escorted by a number of* pashas [generals]. *Despite the fact that each carriage door was masked by a small screen and the body of a black eunuch, enabling the women to look out but not to be seen, the crowd was instructed to look away. These two carriages were followed by twelve more carrying the female servants of the harem, and many litters and four wagons filled with ice and provisions for the women."*[106]

Philanthropist

Philanthropy and patronage of monumental public works were other aspects of the *valide sultan*'s role. Queen mothers played an important role in the construction of public buildings like mosque complexes, hospitals, public baths, soup kitchens for the poor, schools, libraries, fountains, and so on. They also set up endowments to cover the maintenance expenses and salaries of personnel to run the public works. All of these, of course, required huge expenditures. There were several sources of income the *valide sultan* could count upon. The most important were land grants and tax income from royal domains assigned to the queen mother by the sultan or by her son when he became sultan. The immensity of this income can be easily understood when the endowments these women made are examined. They bequeathed whole villages, extensive agricultural land, orchards, vineyards, lemon and olive groves, islands, mines, forts, factories, buildings, *han*s [business center], shops and other business enterprises. The following endowment deed, just one among fourteen trusts set up by the Queen Mother Bezm-i Alem (d. 1852), gives an example of the vast wealth at the command of the *valide sultan*s. These properties were to be used to secure income for the hospital, bath and mosque the queen mother had built:

- one garden and nine shops in Istanbul
- 25,240 olive trees in Edremid and Kemer Edremid
- sixty-three olive oil factories in Edremid and Kemer Edremid
- land called Avcı Koru in the sanjak of Kocaeli
- a pasture called Alacık, a lake, a grocer's shop, and a lot called Balaban Burnu in the town of Terkos
- a meadow called Silahdar and a few fields

- four inns and seven shops in Istanbul
- thirty-seven shares in Ağa Han and one lot in Istanbul
- an island called Hurşidler near Rhodes
- a farm in Varna
- four mulberry orchards and one water mill in Gemlik
- one meadow, two farms and forty-three fields in Istanbul
- the farm called Katip Efendi in Istanbul
- one *han*, four shops, six *donum*s of vineyards, and a half share of one lot in Istanbul
- a field measuring twenty-seven-and-a-half *donum*s, five vineyards, and a half share of one lot in Istanbul
- a coal cellar in Istanbul[107]

In addition to the enormous revenues from land grants and taxes available to the *valide sultan*, she also received other monies and valuable personal goods such as jewelry, objects decorated with precious stones and luxurious material. The queen mother's stipend alone, if calculated at 3,000 aspers a day, amounts to 1,095,000 aspers a year. She also received gifts from the sultan or others on important days like religious holidays, royal celebrations, and other important occasions, and from foreign powers as well.[108] Their great wealth combined with a desire to patronize pious works resulted in significant monument building by the *valide sultan*s. The following are the major examples of *valide sultan*s sponsoring imperial building:

Hafsa Sultan (d. 1534), consort to Sultan Selim I and mother of Sultan Süleyman, built a mosque complex near Manisa, which had been the provincial post her son had been assigned to as a prince. The complex consisted of a mosque (Sultaniye), a religious college, a primary school, a soup kitchen and a dervish hostel. Later a public bath and hospital were added by Sultan Süleyman in his mother's name.[109] Hafsa Sultan was the first *valide sultan* to build an imperial mosque. She was buried next to Sultan Selim's tomb.

Nurbanu Sultan, chief consort to Selim II and mother of Murad III, is thought to be of either Jewish or Italian origin. She constructed another important mosque complex, which was completed in 1583. The mosque was endowed with a library, the first to be established in Istanbul by a woman. This complex included a mosque, a religious college, a school for

Gülnuş Sultan
(1647–1715)

the study of prophetic tradition, an asylum, a primary school, a school to teach reading to the illiterate, and a hospital. There was also a hostel for travelers and a soup kitchen. Nurbanu Sultan also endowed the library with a number of books including Qur'ans with beautiful calligraphy and gilding. She died in 1583 and was buried in the tomb of Selim II in the yard of Ayasofya Mosque [Hagia Sophia].[110]

Mahpeyker Sultan (Kösem Sultan) was consort to Ahmet I and mother of Murad IV and Ibrahim. She built the Çinili Mosque complex in Üsküdar, which included a primary school, fountain, a school for the study of prophetic tradition and a public bath. She also built the Valide Han, a large commercial building, as an endowment for the mosque complex and a *masjid* [a small place of worship] in Anadolu Kavağı. In addition to these, Kösem Sultan endowed a number of other pious works such as helping the poor and providing dowries for orphaned girls. Every year during the holy month of Rajab, this queen mother would dress in disguise, go to the prisons and pay off the debts of imprisoned debtors or pay recompense for crimes other than murder, thus enabling the prisoners to go free. She also had water and sherbet provided to Muslim pilgrims to Mecca, and she arranged for the recitation of the Qur'an in the presence of the Sultan on the day the pilgrim caravan was to depart from Istanbul. Upon her death in 1651, Kösem Sultan was buried in the tomb of Ahmet I next to the Sultanahmet Mosque.[111]

Turhan Sultan, consort to Sultan Ibrahim and mother of Mehmed IV, was born in Russia in 1627. She was captured in a raid made by Tatars and brought to Istanbul at the age of twelve. She became *valide sultan* in 1648 when her son became sultan. Among her charitable works are the completion of the New Mosque, which had been begun in 1598 by Safiye Sultan, a primary school, a school for teaching prophetic traditions, a baazar, a fountain and a tomb. She also built two castles on the Çanakkale Straits, which were endowed with mosques, schools, houses, shelters, and shops. In order to finance her good works, Turhan Sultan bequeathed three bakeries, four shops and large mortars for grinding coffee and some lots of land in Istanbul and forty villages and five farms in Rumelia. In addition, she bequeathed 5,200 piasters for the purchase of land, farms and other property in Anatolia. In addition to stipulating how much money should be paid in salaries to the many employees of these works, the queen mother also stipulated that 3,000 aspers be spent for wood and coal for the students in the winter and 3,000 for taking the students on trips in the summer, 20,000 for the purchase of snow for the fountain house in summer, and 12,000 for rice, onions and firewood for the poor during the holy month of Ramadan. Turhan Sultan designated 7,500 piasters for renting camels to carry pilgrims' belongings and water on the way to the holy pilgrimage and other monies for candles, lamps and olive oil for mosques and for the salaries of those who lit the lamps on holy nights.[112] She died in 1682 and was buried in the tomb she had built next to the mosque.

Gülnuş Sultan, consort to Sultan Mehmed IV and mother of Mustafa II and Ahmed III, was born in Girit of Greek origin. She was captured as a slave girl during the conquest of Girit and sent to the imperial Ottoman palace. Mehmed IV and Gülnuş were mutually captivated and she became the sultan's favorite consort. She often accompanied him on his hunting expeditions for which he was famous.[113] The queen mother had a mosque built in Galata during the reign of her elder son Mustafa II and another mosque built in Üsküdar during the reign of Ahmed III. She also endowed a hospital, a kitchen for the poor, warehouses, a bakery, and mills in Mecca, ships and boats for use at Suez, twenty-one villages in Egypt, and numerous bridges and fountains on the pilgrimage route and elsewhere. She bequeathed some books to the Üsküdar mosque. Gülnuş Sultan died in 1715 in Edirne and after being brought to Istanbul, her body was buried in a tomb next to the mosque she had built in Üsküdar.[114]

◀ Mihrişah Sultan Fountain, 1801

Mihrişah Sultan, consort to Mustafa III and mother of Selim III, is said to be of Georgian origin. She had many fountains built and repaired, and she built the Mihrişah Sultan Mosque and a tomb, primary school and fountain in the district of Eyup. This queen mother also bequeathed some books to the mosque library and extensive property to serve as income for the good works she established. She died in 1805 and was buried in the tomb she had built in Eyup.[115]

Nakşidil Sultan, consort to Abdülhamid I and mother of Mahmud II, built several fountains and a tomb, which is one of the best architectural examples of that period. She became ill while her son was still sultan. She died in 1817 and is buried in the tomb she had built in the Fatih district.[116]

Ayşe Sineperver Sultan, consort to Abdülhamit I and mother of Mustafa IV, reigned as queen mother for only one year before her son was removed from the throne. She endowed a primary school, a fountain, a spring of fresh water and spigots. As income to these endowments, Ayşe Sineperver Sultan bequeathed "four shops, three stone troughs, truck gardens, fields, houses, barns and a big farm together with all its outbuildings and livestock in Istanbul; and in the district of Eyüp, a *han*, a big inn and four farms."[117] She died in 1828 and is buried in Eyup.

Bezm-i Alem Sultan, consort to Mahmud II and mother of Sultan Abdülmecid, is a *valide sultan* who sponsored the construction of many public works. Among her extensive philanthropic works are the Gureba Hospital (1843), a mosque, including a library, and

Pertevniyal Valide Mosque, 1871

fountain near the hospital (1845), a school that is today's Istanbul Girls High School (1850) and a bequest of four-hundred and thirty-one books to the school; the Dolmabahçe Mosque (1853), the Valide Fountain (1839) and a number of other fountains, and the Galata Bridge (1845).[118] She bequeathed extensive property and income to the works she had constructed. She died in 1852 and was buried in the tomb of Sultan Mahmud II.

Pertevniyal Sultan, consort to Mahmud II and mother of Sultan Abdülaziz, reigned as *valide sultan* from 1861 to 1876. She had a mosque (Valide Sultan Mosque), a library, a primary school, a clock room (*muvakkıthane*), a tomb, a mosque in Konya and several fountains built. She bequeathed three hundred and twenty-nine hand-written books and five hundred and fifty-seven printed books to the library in Aksaray. She died in 1882 and was buried in the tomb she had constructed in the district of Aksaray.[119]

Royal Wives and Concubines

Ottoman sultans took both legal wives and slave concubines until the middle of the fifteenth century. From that time forward, with a few notable exceptions, the sultans chose only slave concubines as mates. Although these women did not have noble lineage and were not legal spouses, they had the social status of wife and were called *kadın* or *kadın efendi*. Once a sultan chose a slave woman for his harem, she would be assigned a private room or suite of rooms and personal servants. She was taught palace etiquette by a *kalfa* (a senior female palace official) and new clothing would be ordered for her. A *kadın*'s rank was determined by the order in which she was chosen by the sultan, and it did not change unless a vacancy occurred among the royal consorts due to death or divorce. The first *kadın* or *başkadın* as she was called had a larger retinue and stipend than the other women. The number of royal wives was usually, but not always, limited to the canonical number of four; however, because they were not legally wives, this restriction was not always respected.

Beginning in the latter part of the seventeenth century and continuing through the nineteenth century, in addition to the *kadın*s, the sultans also took concubines called *ikbal*s, who were ranked below the *kadın*s and who were also ranked according to the order in which they were chosen by the sultan. If a vacancy arose among the *kadın*s, the first *ikbal* was moved up to *kadın* status.[120] The *ikbal*s had personal servants as well and were allowed to wear fur-lined clothing during the winter season, indicative of their high status. The number of official consorts a sultan had ranged from eighteen in the case of Ahmed III to none in the case of Mustafa I.[121] However, some sultans also had consorts called *odalık*s, who were not

Melkon, *Beşiktaş Palace*

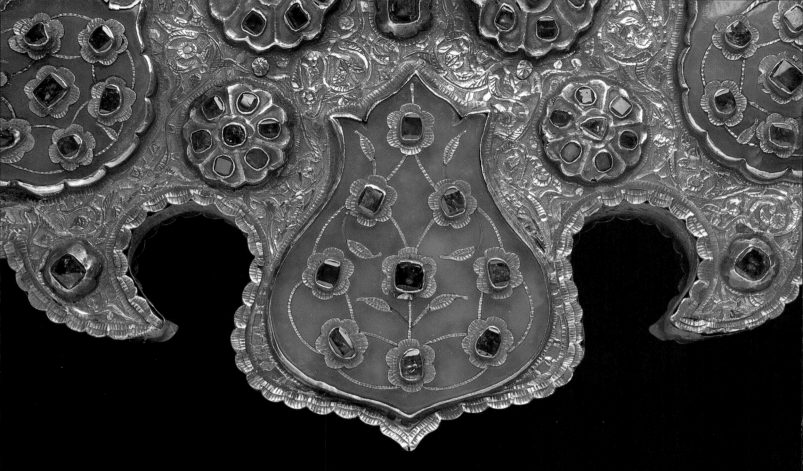

raised to an official rank. Murad III, for example, had only four wives listed,[122] but at the time of his death he had twenty sons and twenty-seven daughters.[123]

Haseki was a title used for favorite concubines of the sultans. The high status of the *haseki* in the harem is indicated by the exceptionally large daily stipend she received in comparison to non-*haseki* concubines. For example, at the end of her career, Hürrem, *haseki* of Sultan Süleyman, received the highest stipend any royal concubine ever received—2,000 aspers a day. The customary amount received by a royal consort who was a mother of a prince at that time was thirty or forty aspers. Nurbanu, *haseki* of Selim II, received one thousand aspers per day (the customary *haseki* stipend), while Selim's other consorts, who were also mothers of sons, received only forty aspers. By the middle of the seventeenth century, the high status of the *haseki* began to diminish and the extreme stipend differences among royal concubines decreased to a more equitable level.[124]

In addition to a daily stipend, the royal concubines also received daily food allowances. For example, in the year 1126 (Hijri calendar) the *kadın*s each received "five *okka*s of meat, three chickens, two *okka*s of oil, a *denk* of snow in the summer, a plate of cream, four loaves of bread, 200 *dirhem*s of honey, compote, one *okka* of fruit, two eggs, four *piliç* (young chickens) and vegetables in season."[125] The young princes and princesses ate with their mothers and sometimes the head *kalfa* ate with her mistress as well. The royal wives also received a supply of candles, soap, wood and coal twice a year and a supply of sugar and coffee.

The royal consorts received annual allowances of clothing material, as did all the residents of the harem. The quality and quantity of their allowance was greater, of course, than that of the common slave girls. Beyazid II, for example, gave his wives 15,000 akçes, nine pieces of European cloth and two sable coats each year.[126] The royal women all dressed in elegant costumes adorned with many precious stones, and they wore valuable jewelry like diamonds, emeralds and rubies. Lady Montague's detailed description of her own Turkish costume gives us a good idea of courtly Ottoman female dress:

"The first part of my dress is a pair of drawers, very full, that reach to my shoes, and conceal the legs more modestly than your petticoats. They are of a thin rose-coloured damask, brocaded with silver flowers. My shoes are of white kid leather, embroidered with gold. Over this hangs my smock, of a fine white silk gauze, edged with embroidery. This smock has wide sleeves, hanging half-way down the arm, and is closed at the neck with a diamond button; but the shape and colour of the bosom are very well to be distinguished through it. The 'antery' is a waistcoat, made close to the shape, of white and gold damask, with very long sleeves falling back, and fringed with deep gold fringe, and should have diamond or pearl buttons. My 'caftan,' of the same stuff with my drawers, is a robe exactly fitted to my shape, and reaching to my feet, with very long strait falling sleeves. Over this is my girdle, of about four fingers broad, which all that can afford it have entirely of diamonds or other precious stones; those who will not be at that expense have it of exquisite embroidery on satin; but it must be fastened

before with a clasp of diamonds. The 'curdee' is a loose robe they throw off or put on according to the weather, being of a rich brocade (mine is green and gold,)[127] *either lined with ermine or sables; the sleeves reach very little below the shoulders. The headdress is composed of a cap, called 'talpock,' which is in winter of fine velvet, embroidered with pearls or diamonds, and in summer of a light shining silver stuff. This is fixed on one side of the head, hanging a little way down with a gold tassel, and bound on, either with a circle of diamonds (as I have seen several) or a rich embroidered handkerchief. On the other side of the head, the hair is laid flat; and here the ladies are at liberty to show their fancies; some putting flowers, others a plume of heron's feathers, and, in short, what they please; but the most general fashion is a large bouquet of jewels, made like natural flowers; that is, the buds, of pearl; the roses, of different coloured rubies; the jessamines, of diamonds; the jonquils, of topazes, etc. so well set and enameled, it is hard to imagine anything of that kind so beautiful. The hair hangs at its full length behind, divided into tress braided with pearl or ribbon, which is always in great quantity."*

In addition to allowances of food, clothing and fuel and daily stipends, the royal concubines also received significant gifts. One type of gift was revenue from crown lands, similar to but usually much less than income received by the *valide sultan*. Another type of gift was that received on special occasions like weddings of the sultan's daughters, circumcisions of his sons, holy days, returns from conquest, and so on. These gifts might be made by the sultan, by other members of the royal family, by high-level

◀ Osman III Kiosk, Topkapı Palace   Lady's dress (*üçetek entari*) ▶

military men or by foreign officials. Sometimes the gift was in the form of money, but it might also be jewelry, rich material, furs or valuable ornaments.

Although the apartments of the royal concubines were not as large and as splendid as the queen mother's, they were, nevertheless, luxuriously and comfortably furnished. According to Leyla Saz, who spent long periods of time at Çırağan Imperial Palace, the *kadın*s and *ikbal*s had two rooms each on the second floor of the palace, one facing the Bosphorus Straits and serving as a salon and one facing the palace gardens and serving as a bedroom. The rooms on the first floor underneath the bedrooms of the royal consorts were occupied by their *kalfa*s. There were stairs built into cupboards in these rooms that enabled the *kalfa*s to attend their mistresses without using the main staircase in the palace. In addition, there were auxiliary rooms that supported these apartments such as bathrooms, and dressing rooms, which were sometimes private and sometimes shared in common by the women.[128]

The royal wives spent much time carefully supervising the education and training of their children and their finances. In their spare time they read the Qur'an and literary works and busied themselves with handicrafts and music.[129] There were also indoor palace activities like musical and dance performances once or twice a week. The musically talented slave girls were trained by the best musicians available, and they would give regular performances for the royal family and harem residents. In the nineteenth century the all-female harem orchestra played both Turkish and Western music. There were also promenades in the extensive palace gardens during the spring and summer. Leyla Saz describes such an outing:

"When the Sultan authorised a promenade in the gardens of the Mabeyin, the gardeners and the watchmen withdrew and soldiers were placed outside at intervals along the walls, then the eunuchs shouted: 'Halvette! Halvette! Halvette! or 'Withdraw! Silence!' in order to chase away anyone still present. At that point, the gates of the bridge with the grills were simultaneously opened along with the gates of a corridor which led from the Serail [Palace] to the garden of the Harem. Then everyone entered the park.

"First, the little princes and the little princesses, sometimes even the Sultan himself, slowly crossed the bridge followed by their Great Kalfas and the girls of the service which were directly attached to them; then came all the other girls of the Serail with the exception of those who were on duty. They poured in like a torrent and spread throughout this immense park where

they frolicked about freely, running from flower to flower like butterflies, climbing the trees, leaping and dashing about, and having no idea of the passage of time."[130]

Another kind of favorite outing was an excursion to Kağıthane or the Sweet Waters of Europe. The sultan would authorize all the ladies of the imperial harem to participate in these promenades a number of times during the spring and summer seasons. A long line of imperial carriages carrying the *kadın*s and princesses would be formed according to protocol. This would be followed by an even longer line of regular carriages carrying the *kalfa*s and attendant slave girls. The procession would proceed to pavilions at the Sweet Waters where the ladies would stop and perform their midday prayer. They would be served fruit and yogurt by the watchmen of the pavilions and the eunuchs. The royal women would sometimes sit among their attendants and watch the waterfalls.[131]

The royal consorts also participated in many palace celebrations on both holy days and royal occasions like births, weddings of the princesses and circumcisions. The following is a description of the Ramadan palace ceremony at which all the women of the imperial harem paid their respects to the sultan:

"*The music* [played by the harem orchestra consisting of eighty female musicians] *played the air of salute while the Sultan made his entry having on his left the* haznedar usta *and followed by those women who were in his particular service and all wearing the uniform of their rank.*

"*His Majesty arrived in front of the door and* Valide Sultan *placed herself at his side; the music then struck up the Imperial March.*

"*The sultanes, the* hanım sultanes *or the daughters of* sultanes *then arrived in order of age, advancing slowly with a manner both majestic and respectful, letting their skirts trail behind them on the parquet. They approached His Majesty and made a grand reverence to the floor and then arranged themselves on his right, while keeping their hands crossed on their chest in the traditional attitude of respect. Then came the consorts recognised by the Sultan, the* kadıns *and* ikbals *who placed themselves on his left in the same fashion. The old* kalfas *or* haznedars, *who the* sultanes *had taken with them, then approached in their turn, kissed the floor and then arranged themselves far off in a corner. The music never stopped playing during the whole ceremony.*

"At this point, two young girls carried in a silk napkin woven with gold and containing small brand new coins, which the haznedar usta *took in handfuls and threw around the hall. The* kalfas *of a medium rank who watched from afar this whole ceremony, only picked up those coins which rolled near them but the little ones darted around on all sides like the pigeons around the mosques, which fall upon the seeds which are thrown to them. Among these little girls, there would sometimes be one bold enough to approach close to the Sultan, who would only smile at her with indulgence."*[132]

Hürrem Sultan

One of the most famous royal concubines is Hürrem Sultan, who was a *haseki* (favorite) of Sultan Süleyman. She was the daughter of a Polish priest and is known in Western sources as Roxelana. Süleyman greatly loved Hürrem and eventually made her his legal wife, in contradiction to the custom of royal concubinage at the time. So great was the Sultan's dedication to Hürrem that he forewent all other sexual partners. Hürrem bore him five sons, also in contradiction to the custom of one mother-one prince. Prince Mustafa, son to Süleyman and his first consort, Mahidevran Hatun, was the only rival to Hürrem's sons. Mustafa, greatly loved by the people, was eventually executed by his father on charges of treason, allegedly at the instigation of Hürrem, her daughter Mihrimah and son-in-law Rüstem Paşa. Hürrem's suspected involvement in Mustafa's execution made her unpopular with the people. However, she sponsored a number of significant public works:

"Major philanthropic institutions existed in her name in Mecca, Medina, and Jerusalem, the holiest cities of the Islamic world, and in Istanbul and Edirne, the principal seats of the Ottoman sultanate after 1453. The earliest of these, the Istanbul complex, constructed between 1537 and 1539, consisted of a mosque, a religious college, a soup kitchen, a hospital, and a primary school. The well-endowed complex in Jerusalem, completed in the early 1550s, contained a mosque, a fifty-five room dwelling for religious pilgrims, an area devoted to charitable services for the poor (including a bakery, soup kitchen, storeroom, and public toilets), and an inn and stable for travelers. The Edirne complex consisted of a mosque, soup kitchen, and inn."[133]

Hürrem Sultan (1506–1558)

Upon the succession of a new sultan to the throne, the royal concubines, together with their children, were removed to the older palaces, which were places of retirement for royal concubines and places of training for new slave girls. If the royal consort was the mother of a prince, she might at a later date return to the New Palace as the *valide sultan*. If not, she spent the rest of her days in the Old Palace. Childless *ikbal*s or *odalik*s were usually married off to men of the ruling elite.

Princesses

Ottoman princesses were also called sultan, but their title was put after their first name. These women were born into a world of majesty and magnificence. From the moment a princess opened her eyes, she was surrounded by splendor. The royal family ceremonially celebrated the births of both princes and princesses. A large room in the imperial harem would be set aside for the royal birth and decorated in a manner that clearly reflected the magnificence of the Ottoman court. The cradle and the mother's bed were furnished with new luxurious covers decorated with pearls, jewels and gold and silver thread. Curtains, divan covers and their cushions were made from the best material and decorated with sequins and gold and silver embroidery worked into beautiful designs. There were also silver and gilded brass basins and ewers to be used during the birth. The cradle, sometimes made from gold, would be decorated with valuable jewels. The outlay of money for royal births was often huge. Many valuable gifts were given, and the palace was illuminated with oil lamps and lanterns, as were the mansions of high state officials. Public celebrations sometimes lasted seven days during which the people were entertained with fireworks, tumblers and acrobats. Ottoman state officials and the people were informed of royal births by cannon fire. The birth of a princess was announced with the firing of five cannon balls and the birth of a prince with seven. Edicts were also sent throughout the Empire announcing the royal birth.[134]

There were two important cradle processions, the first of which was the *valide sultan* procession. The queen mother would have the cradle and covers for the new prince or princess made and sent to the Old Palace. They would be brought to Topkapı Palace by means of a procession of palace officials. As the procession passed along the streets, the people would pray for blessings for the new baby and the sultan. When the cradle arrived at Topkapı Palace, it would be taken to the room prepared for the royal birth. The second procession, the Grand Vizier's Cradle Procession, took place on the sixth day after the birth, and it was an even more magnificent event. The Grand Vizier would have an expensive cradle and cradle covers made, which were carried to Topkapı Palace in a huge procession in tune to music played by the military band. The officials who participated in the procession were given caftans, fur coats, other kinds of apparel and material according to their rank. The cradle and covers were taken first to the sultan for his inspection and then to the room where the royal birth had taken place. The *kadın efendi*s, *ikbal*s and the wives of all the officials who had been invited to the procession would be seated according to their rank, while the *valide sultan* sat on a chair accompanied by the other princesses. The midwife who had delivered the baby would put it in the cradle, rock it three times, and make special prayers for the infant. After she took it to her lap again, the guests put valuable material and jewels into the cradle, all of which went to the midwife. The women then presented valuable gifts to the new baby and its mother. Music and dancing would begin and the guests would be entertained for three days in the imperial harem.[135]

The new princess was assigned a separate apartment and provided with a wet nurse, a governess, a *kalfa* and attendants. Her mother, governess and *kalfa* trained the princess and

◀ Dürrüşehvar Sultan ▲
(1914–2006)

125

oversaw her activities. Often small slave girls were assigned to play with her and, under the auspices of her governess or *kalfa*, the princess and her little friends would play in the palace gardens. When she became of school age, teachers were assigned to teach the young princess. According to Ayşe Sultan, daughter of Abdülhamit II, two teachers were assigned to her and her sister, Şadiye Sultan. One taught the Qur'an, Arabic and Persian, and the other taught the princesses Turkish reading and writing, Ottoman rules and regulations, mathematics, history and geography. Ayşe Sultan wrote that all the palace residents met them at the door of the harem and wished them success. After their first lesson, the princesses went to kiss the hand of their father, who, after kissing them on the forehead, encouraged the girls to study hard.[136] Leyla Saz wrote that all the princesses were excellent musicians.[137]

Although the princesses received smaller stipends than the royal consorts when they were young, which suggests a lower status in the harem, their position in protocol was higher than that of the *kadın efendi*s and *ikbal*s. At the Ramadan holiday ceremony in the imperial harem, the princesses preceded the royal consorts in paying respects to the sultan, and they stood on the sultan's right side while the concubines stood to his left.[138] Also, when they married, their stipends were greatly increased and they were given ample household allowances and their own palace or mansion.[139] The princesses also had more freedom than did other palace women. They were allowed to make calls on the wives of viziers and to shop and promenade. Saz describes the shopping event as follows:

Bowl (*şifa tast*).
18th century

"In those days the main street of the Bazaar was accessible to carriages. The princesses and the ladies of the Imperial Harem were allowed to go there and they did go from time to time, but it was not considered suitable to stop in front of the shops, much less to enter them. They would install themselves in the mosque of Nuruosmaniye, in a part of the building especially reserved for the Sultan and the Imperial Family, just as there is in every one of the Grand Mosques of Istanbul. The shopkeepers, advised by the people of the suite of the princess, would bring their merchandise to them and, in turn, these would be presented

126

Mehmed IV Pavilion, Topkapı Palace

to the princesses by the eunuchs. The princess would then make her choice, the material would be cut into the appropriate sizes and other articles desired would be put to one side and then the eunuch would settle accounts with the merchant."[140]

The weddings of the princesses were usually very lavish affairs. Until the mid-fifteenth century, Ottoman sultans married their daughters and sisters to Muslim rulers and their sons or to members of the Ottoman ruling class. After that, princesses were married only to members of the elite ruling class or in some cases to cousins. Frequently they were married to viziers or other important men such as the chief of the Admiralty, alliances that greatly enhanced their influence. Men who were chosen as royal sons-in-law had to divorce any previous wives they might have. They also gave up their right to divorce. A princess could divorce her husband (with the sultan's consent), but a princess' husband could not initiate divorce. Marrying a princess was a very expensive affair because of the many valuable gifts that had to be given to the royal family and because of the princess' palace, which was sometimes provided by the son-in-law. On the other hand, the husband of a princess benefited greatly by such a marriage. He was almost certain to be promoted to a higher office, and his power and wealth increased considerably through his association with the royal family. The following list of engagement gifts presented to Fatma Sultan, daughter of Ahmed III, by the Sultan's Sword Bearer, Ali Paşa, gives an idea of the great expense incurred by a royal son-in-law and the value placed on marriage to a princess:

- a Qur'an with a jeweled binding and jeweled cloth case
- a ring in a jeweled box
- a gold tray
- a jeweled crown
- a jeweled *istefan*
- a jeweled silver belt
- a jeweled bracelet
- a jeweled aigrette
- a jeweled veil
- jeweled bath thongs
- a pair of shoes adorned with pearls
- a sable coat
- a pair of diamond earrings
- 15 bags of new coins and *akça*s
- 2 silver *nahil*s
- 120 trays of candy
- 2 'flower gardens'
- 5 bundles containing miscellaneous items
- brocade cloth
- 7 silver trays

On the day of the engagement, members of the imperial council were invited to Sofa Mansion by Sultan Ahmed III to view Fatma Sultan's trousseau, which was later taken to her new home in a grand procession. The large baskets and trunks were loaded on fifty-five mules and a number of closed carriages. The more valuable objects were carried by hand in a large procession of palace officers and halberdiers. On the day of the engagement the groom-to-be gave the following gifts:

- Grand Vizier—a new jeweled girdle and a jeweled aigrette
- Sheikhulislam—a Qur'an and a jeweled watch
- General—a pair of diamond bracelets
- High Admiral—a jeweled girdle
- General—a jeweled girdle
- Rumelia Chief Military Judge—20 gold pieces
- Anatolia Chief Military Judge—watch set with rubies
- Janissary Agha—a jeweled girdle
- Minister of Finance—a pair of jeweled bracelets

In addition, Ali Paşa had sent other valuable gifts to the bride, the Sultan, his wives and the Chief Eunuch that included horses, jewels, jeweled girdles, valuable books, prayer rugs, rosaries and fur skins. The Sultan, on the other hand, made Ali Paşa a vizier and appointed him as the Deputy Grand Vizier.

On the day of the wedding, Fatma Sultan went to her new home in a silver carriage in a huge, colorful procession that included all the ministers, scholars and state officials as well as the hundreds of halberdiers and palace officials that had been in the trousseau procession. There were thirty-one carriages of palace women as well. The officials all wore magnificent caftans and uniforms, and the horses were decked out exquisitely. Colorful pieces of cloth were tied around the necks of animals pulling the carriages, and splendid wreaths were carried by halberdiers. Ten bags of gold coins were thrown to the crowds as the procession slowly moved through the streets of Istanbul. The people prayed for the Sultan and gave good wishes to the bride. After the procession reached its destination, feasting and entertainment began. There were games, contests, music, dancing, acrobatic displays and fireworks.

Interestingly, all these lavish celebrations were only symbolic because Fatma Sultan was only five years old at the time of her engagement. Ali Paşa waited eight years for Fatma

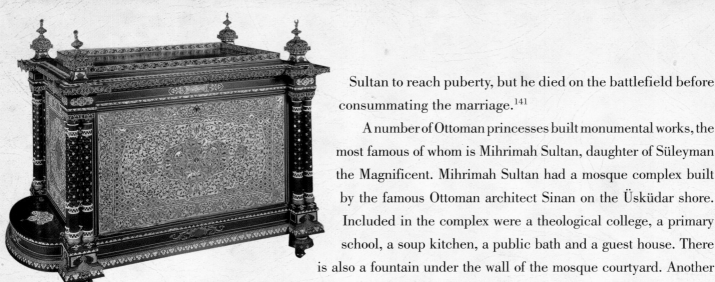

Jewelry chest.
Dolmabahçe Palace

Sultan to reach puberty, but he died on the battlefield before consummating the marriage.[141]

A number of Ottoman princesses built monumental works, the most famous of whom is Mihrimah Sultan, daughter of Süleyman the Magnificent. Mihrimah Sultan had a mosque complex built by the famous Ottoman architect Sinan on the Üsküdar shore. Included in the complex were a theological college, a primary school, a soup kitchen, a public bath and a guest house. There is also a fountain under the wall of the mosque courtyard. Another mosque complex was built in her name in the Edirnekapı district, which included a theological college, a primary school and a double public bath. Sinan was also the architect of this mosque. This princess was dearly loved by her father, and she was buried in his tomb at the Süleymaniye Mosque when she died in 1556.[142] Ismihan Sultan, granddaughter of Sultan Süleyman and daughter of Sultan Selim II and Nurbanu Sultan, had a theological college built by Sinan in 1569–70. It included a library containing four hundred and thirty volumes. She also had a church rebuilt into a mosque in the Sultanahmed Square. Her husband Sokullu Mehmed Paşa added a theological college, a fountain and a dervish lodge to the mosque. This princess died two days after childbirth in 1585, and she is buried in her father's tomb at the Ayasofya Mosque.[143] Zeyneb Sultan, daughter of Sultan Selim III, had a small mosque complex constructed in 1769 across from the gate of Gülhane Park. It included a primary school, a fountain and a tomb in addition to the mosque. Dying in 1774, this princess was buried in the tomb she had built.[144]

Daye Hatun (Sultan's Wet Nurse)

It was the custom for Ottoman princes and princesses to be nursed by wet nurses, whose own children would be considered as *sütkardeşleri* (milk brothers or sisters) to the royal children. These women had a high status in the imperial harem and would fulfill the ceremonial role of the sultan's mother if his natural mother died before he did. The wet nurses were shown great respect by the sultans and were given generous grants. They frequently used these endowments to construct public buildings like mosques and masjids. These women were often married to statesmen. For example, Sultan Mehmet III married his wet nurse Halime Hatun to his former mentor and Grand Vizier, Lala Mehmed Paşa.[145]

Kethüda Hatun (Harem Stewardess)

The harem stewardess was the senior administrative officer in the imperial harem, and she would be chosen by the sultan for this position because of her experience, knowledge and refinement. She directed all the ceremonies in the harem and trained women as to how to behave towards the sultan and the royal family. Her high status is reflected by the fact that only she, the sultan and the grand vizier carried the imperial seal and by the fur coat that was bestowed upon her at her appointment. Both she and the sultan's wet nurse are included as members of the royal family in the privy registers. Apparently, the harem stewardess also had the means to undertake public works. For example, Canfeda Hatun, harem stewardess under Murad III, built a mosque and a fountain in Istanbul and another mosque and public bath in a nearby village.[146]

Administrative Staff

After the royal women, the *kalfa*s were next in rank in the imperial harem. They were in the personal service of the sultan. The following are examples of their positions:[147]

• *Haznedar Usta* (Treasurer). The Head Treasurer would attend the sultan when he was in the harem. The other four *haznedar usta*s and their assistants would guard the door to the sultan's room day and night. They also looked after the sultan's clothing and jewels and the general harem economy. They had a staff of approximately twenty assistant *kalfa*s.

• *Çeşnigir Usta* (Lady Butler). She and her staff of *kalfa*s and assistants oversaw the sultan's food and table service. She would taste the food first to make sure it was not poisoned, and then present it to the sultan.

Turkish woman. Levni's collage (*murakka*)

Çamaşırcı Usta (Head Laundress). She would supervise the laundering of the sultan's clothing in the basement of the palace. During the reign of Sultan Abdülhamid II, the clothing was washed in seven silver basins, hung to dry on lines in the garden used only for the Sultan's laundry and then ironed by the laundry staff.

- *İbriktâr Usta* (Mistress of the Sultan's Ewer). She and her staff were in charge of the sultan's water pitcher, basin and towels. They would also pour water for the sultan's ablutions and for washing his face and hands.

- *Berber Usta* (Mistress of the Sultan's Shaving Equipment). She and her staff oversaw the sultan's shaving equipment.

- *Kahveci Usta* (Coffee Mistress). She and her staff made and served coffee to the sultan. On ceremonial occasions they served coffee to the *kadın*s and female guests who came to pay their respects to the sultan.

- *Kilerci Usta* (Mistress of the Sultan's Pantry). Fresh and dried fruit and sherbets made for the sultan were stored in the pantry. This *kalfa* and her staff oversaw the pantry and served pantry items to the sultan. She also served the sultan during his meals.

- *Kutucu Usta* (Mistress of Headdresses). She and her staff assisted the sultans, *kadınefendi*s and *ikbal*s in their bathing and dressing. They also assisted in hairdressing and oversaw headdresses.

- *Külhane Usta* (Mistress of the Baths). She and her staff lit the stoves in the baths and washed the sultan's odalisques.

- *Katibe Usta* (Head Scribe). She and her staff were responsible for maintaining discipline in the imperial harem. They would control who entered and left the harem and they would monitor all activities in the harem.

- *Hastalar Ustası* (Chief Health Officer). She was the head of the health care staff in the harem.

- *Ebe* (Midwife). There were a number of midwives in the imperial harem who assisted with births and abortions.

- *Dadı* (Governess). A governess and a head *kalfa* were assigned to each of the sultan's children. They raised the child together with its natural mother. The governesses were highly respected in the harem and were often

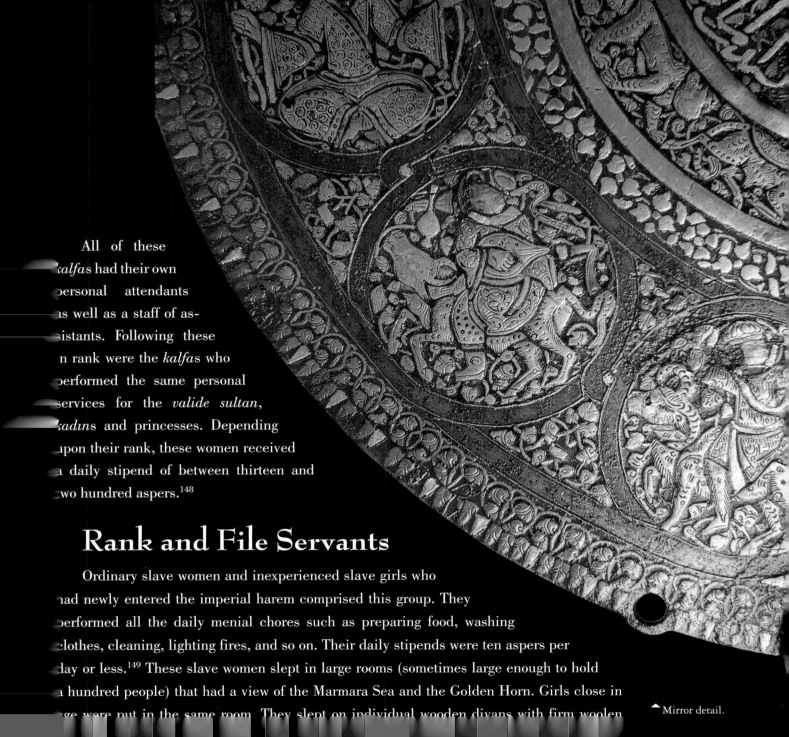

All of these *kalfa*s had their own personal attendants as well as a staff of assistants. Following these in rank were the *kalfa*s who performed the same personal services for the *valide sultan*, *kadın*s and princesses. Depending upon their rank, these women received a daily stipend of between thirteen and two hundred aspers.[148]

Rank and File Servants

Ordinary slave women and inexperienced slave girls who had newly entered the imperial harem comprised this group. They performed all the daily menial chores such as preparing food, washing clothes, cleaning, lighting fires, and so on. Their daily stipends were ten aspers per day or less.[149] These slave women slept in large rooms (sometimes large enough to hold a hundred people) that had a view of the Marmara Sea and the Golden Horn. Girls close in age were put in the same room. They slept on individual wooden divans with firm woolen

▲ Mirror detail.

mattresses. To prevent any kind of trouble, an elderly slave woman slept between every ten girls, and oil lamps burned all night long. The rooms were also patrolled by the *katibe* [female scribe] staff.

As soon as slave girls were brought to the palace, they were taught the basic tenets and practices of Islam, and they were expected to perform the five mandatory prayers a day. They were also taught to read the Qur'an. According to Saz, the women in the imperial harem piously performed their worship:

"The princesses and the ladies of the Serail having received, since their infancy, good religious instruction and having all the attitudes of piety, closely observed all the demands of religion, notably those concerning the five daily prayers and the fast of Ramadan."[150]

All of the slave girls were taught to speak Turkish. Those with the beauty and charm to become potential consorts of the sultan were taught to read and write as well. Those who were musically talented were taught to play instruments, sing and/or dance. The slave girls learned to sew, make lace and knit. In addition, great importance was given to teaching them refined manners. Potential concubines were trained to behave in a way that would become a sultan's wife.

Those slave women who did not become consorts to the sultan or to a prince and who did not want to remain in the administrative staff of the harem could ask for their freedom after nine years of service. They would be given a certificate of manumission, which they usually carried on their person. A husband would be found for them, and they would be given a dowry, often a house and a regular income. They kept their ties with the palace and could expect support from the royal family whenever they needed it for the rest of their lives.

Turkish woman miniature ▶

Favorites' Courtyard. Ladies' apartments. Topkapı Palace

V

Ottoman Women in Court Records

With regard to their legal status, Turkish women ... already possess all the legal, personal, and proprietary rights necessary to give them a social position equal, if not superior to that of European women generally.[151]

Lucy M. Garnett, 1909

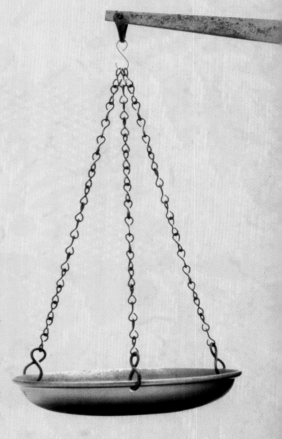

◀ Allom, *The Petition Writer (arzuhalci)*, 1840

A portrait or description of Ottoman women would be incomplete without examining the image of women that emerges from Ottoman court records. European travelers' reports and descriptions of Ottoman women in the imperial and household harems show them in a basically feminine environment or female sphere. The court records, however, reveal the activities of Ottoman women in the legal or public sphere. Scholarship to date overwhelmingly indicates that these women were aware of their legal rights and that they actively pursued their rights in the courts. Mainly women used the courts to settle issues related to marriage and divorce, to secure financial maintenance, to settle personal property issues and to complain about physical violence. In general, they took any kind of problem to court that they were unable to resolve by other means. When they were unable to obtain justice through the local courts, Ottoman women petitioned the Imperial Council in Istanbul for redress of their grievances. Their complaints were recorded in *şikayet defterleri* (complaint registers). Regarding this process, one scholar writes:

"We know that women and minorities appealed to the local shari'ah courts continually, but the Sublime Porte and the imperial council were farther away and out of reach. Despite distance and great hazards, women came from as far as Egypt to petition, showing that the myth of 'royal justice' was widespread and strong enough to convince many, even those from the farthest corners of the Empire, to undertake a laborious journey to Istanbul to present their grievances in person."[152]

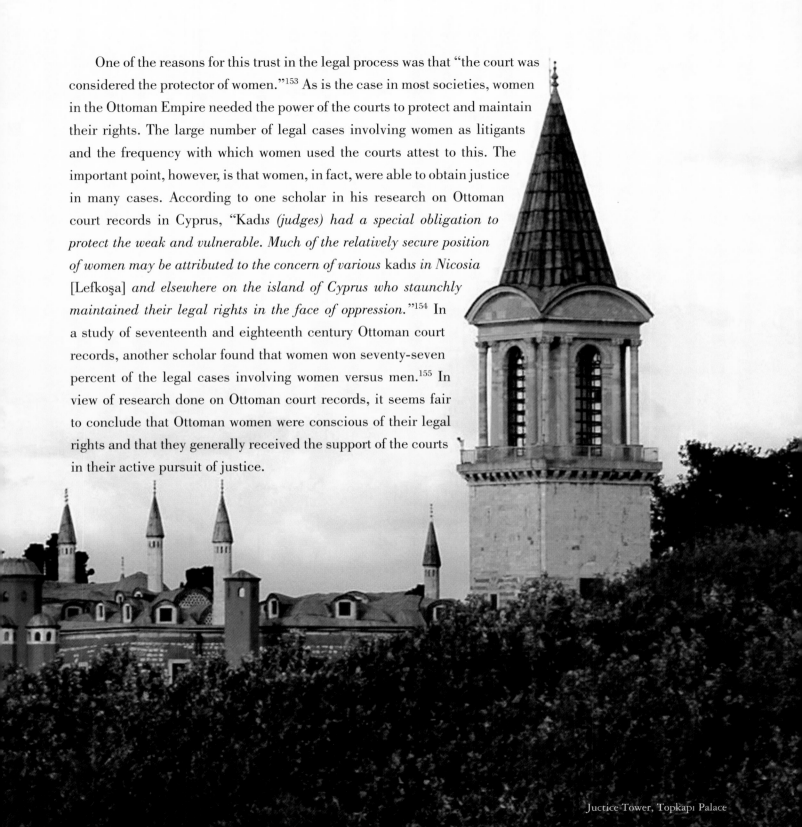

One of the reasons for this trust in the legal process was that "the court was considered the protector of women."[153] As is the case in most societies, women in the Ottoman Empire needed the power of the courts to protect and maintain their rights. The large number of legal cases involving women as litigants and the frequency with which women used the courts attest to this. The important point, however, is that women, in fact, were able to obtain justice in many cases. According to one scholar in his research on Ottoman court records in Cyprus, "Kadıs *(judges) had a special obligation to protect the weak and vulnerable. Much of the relatively secure position of women may be attributed to the concern of various* kadıs *in Nicosia* [Lefkoşa] *and elsewhere on the island of Cyprus who staunchly maintained their legal rights in the face of oppression."*[154] In a study of seventeenth and eighteenth century Ottoman court records, another scholar found that women won seventy-seven percent of the legal cases involving women versus men.[155] In view of research done on Ottoman court records, it seems fair to conclude that Ottoman women were conscious of their legal rights and that they generally received the support of the courts in their active pursuit of justice.

Juctice Tower, Topkapı Palace

Marriage

It was custom for the hand of the girl to be given in marriage by her legal guardian, which was usually her father. However, it could be a grandfather, uncle, brother or other male relative in the absence of the father. In some cases, when there was no such relative, the *kadı* acted as the girl's agent, or a girl of adult age (one who had reached puberty) could be married without any proxy at all. However, consent of the bride was necessary for the marriage to be legally valid. If a girl was an adult, she could immediately complain to the court if she had been married against her will, and the court would annul the marriage. The following is an example from court records of such a case:

"Haci Bola bint Huseyn, of (adult) age, of Salurci Dere village of Amasiyya kaza sets forth a claim saying: On 28 I Cumadi 1034 my father Huseyn married me to Spahi Mehmed Beg. When I heard this, I refused to accept it. I want that marriage cancelled and I want to marry this Ibrahim Çelebi bn Keyvan. I did not give my consent to be married to Mehmed. A fetva [legal opinion] *is presented that she is of age and her father cannot marry her against her wishes...The marriage is annulled and permission is given for her to marry Ibrahim Çelebi. (Amasya sicil I 19–2; selh Cumadi I 1034)"*[156]

When the girl was under age at the time the marriage was contracted, she usually stayed with her parents until she reached puberty, at which time she would go to live with her husband and the marriage would be consummated. If, as an adult, she objected to a marriage that had been contracted for her when she was under age, she could complain to the court and get the marriage annulled. The following is an example:

"Ayşe bint Mustafa Başa: I have come of age. I will not accept the marriage that my uncle Mahmud has arranged. I terminate it. I make Emir Ali Bn Hamdi my vekil *(guardian) for everything. Ali accepts. (20 41–2; 12 Cumadi I 1027)"*[157]

Marriage Contract

In order for a marriage to be legal, the record of marriage had to include the names of the bride, bridegroom, their guardians or agents and the witnesses to the marriage. It also had to include the marriage contract with a designation of the amount of *mahr* (dowry) that was to be given to the bride by the groom and the conditions under which the marriage

Rietschel, *Petition Writers*, 1855–60

was being contracted. The conditions listed in the marriage contract were especially important to the bride because the bridegroom was legally responsible for fulfilling them. This gave women leverage that could later on be brought to bear legally when necessary.

Mahr (Dowry)

One of the conditions that had to be included in the marriage contract was the amount of dowry to be paid by the husband to the bride. The dowry was usually divided into two portions. The *mahr-i mu'ajjal* [prompt] was paid before the consummation of the marriage. The bride did not go to her husband's home until the agreed upon sum had been paid. The *mahr-i mu'ajjal* [deferred] was the delayed sum to be paid to the wife upon divorce or death of the husband. This, of course, served as a deterrent to divorce because the husband was liable for its payment. The details of how much and in what form the dowry was to be paid were clearly recorded in the contract to prevent possible future disputes. Usually it was paid in gold or silver coins, but well-to-do men also gave title deeds and shares of property and jewelry. Unlike the "drahoma," money received by the husband upon marriage, or a bride price paid to the father of the bride, the dowry belonged solely to the bride and could not be used by the groom without her explicit permission. The following is an example of dowry recorded in 1551 in the *sharia* court records in Alexandria, Egypt:

> "*40 silver nisfs were paid to the bride Farhana, who declared she had received half, the other half determined as a delayed dowry. (Jami al-Hakim 957/1551, 1:183–824)*"[158]

Ottoman coins (19th century) and banknote (early 20th century)

* * *

Fatıma, whose husband Ahmed Ağa died, applied to the Istanbul court to claim her dowry right from the deceased's estate, which had been completely confiscated by her mother-in-law and brother-in-law. Above is the ruling that stipulated that the hearing of this case be held in Silivri, where Fatıma and her family resided, in order to resolve the conflict for a fair distribution of the estate among heirs.

Istanbul Court Ruling Records: Istanbul'da Sosyal Hayat 2 (1755–1765) [Social Life in Istanbul], Istanbul Collection IX, Istanbul Research Center, p. 85. Ruling no. 4/71/193.

If the husband refused to pay the wife's dowry as agreed, he could be put in jail. In one particular case in Bursa where the husband didn't give his wife her *mahr-i muʿajjal*, which was to include household items in the amount of 1,015 *kuruş*, he was incarcerated for sixty days.[159]

Other stipulations in the marriage contract often included such matters as the place of the marital residence, the husband's remaining in the marital home, his acceptance of the wife's children from a previous marriage or her mother and his pledge to support them, the husband's refraining from taking another wife or concubine and the husband's provision of a clothing allowance for the wife. Both parties to the contract understood that if the conditions were not met by the husband, his wife could get a divorce without forfeiting her delayed dowry or by forfeiting a portion stipulated in the contract. This was very important to the wife because women who sued for divorce often had to give up their delayed dowry in exchange for their freedom. The following is a typical example of a marriage contract:

"Abu'l-Hassan ibn Ibrahim ibn ʿAbdullah ... married the virgin Ghajariyya bint Khalid ibn Mohammed al-Maghrabi. The contracted mahr was thirty new gold Sultani dinars, of which eight dinars were received by her mother Ward, and twenty-two dinars were designated as mu'akhkhar (delayed). Abu'l-Hassan also committed to pay her six silver ansaf as a monthly clothing allowance and agreed on her following conditions: if he were to take a second wife "in any manner"; if he were to travel more than once a year or move to a far away place for good; or if he were to beat her violently leaving marks; then he would be entitled to withhold no more than a quarter of the remaining dowry, which would be indisputably hers if she chose to divorce him. (al-Barmashiyya 994/1589, 707: 113–711)"[160]

Brindesi, *Passenger Boat in front of the Rumeli Fortress*, 1855

Nafaka (Maintenance Support)

Men were required by law to fully support their wives and children, including food, clothing, shelter, household help, and medical expenses. The amount of support depended on a woman's socio-economic position. This support continued as long as the couple was married and for three months after divorce. The husband was responsible for maintaining his wife even if he were absent from the home or had disappeared, in which case the court would order a loan to be made on his behalf and the wife's support would be paid from the loan, which the husband was legally responsible for.

When the husband refused to pay for her support, his wife could complain to the court and the *kadı* would enforce payment. A typical example is Şerife Emine Hanım of Bursa, who applied to the court when she didn't receive support from her husband and was awarded two hundred kuruş a month as support payment.[161] Another court record from Kayseri contains a claim by Cennet Ana bint Sheik Mehmet Efendi that reads, *"I am the wife of Abdul-Fettah bn Abdul-Kadir of Gulluk mahalle [neighborhood], who has been absent for a long time. I want maintenance allowance. Cennet Ana is asked to take an oath that her husband has allotted nothing for her. Then she is granted fifteen akçe per day and permission to seek a loan (25 48–2; 4 Rebi II 1034)."*[162]

One scholar, who studied Ottoman court records of Kırşehir between the years 1880 and 1906, concluded:

"When the records are examined, many are found which show that the kadı implemented the laws to the letter, that according to the conditions of the times the kadı assigned to women a daily allowance called 'nafaka ve kisve baha,' and the husbands were held responsible for its payment."[163]

The Holy Qur'an cover.
Topkapı Palace Museum

Divorce and Remarriage

The most common form of divorce was *talak* or repudiation of the wife by the husband. Upon a first and second repudiation, the husband could remarry his wife, but the third repudiation was final. After that point, a man could only remarry his wife after she married and divorced another man. In this type of divorce, the wife was entitled to any delayed dowry that had been agreed upon in the marriage contract and to maintenance support during a three-month period in which it was determined whether or not she was pregnant. The husband was also liable for any debts he owed his wife.

Another type of divorce was called *hul*. This could be by mutual agreement or at the request of the wife. If the husband accepted it, the wife usually had to forego any delayed dowry and maintenance payment and, in some cases, she paid him a sum beyond what was owed to her. A woman could also get divorced through the court, even if her husband refused, in the case of violation of the marriage contract, impotence, desertion, failure to support the wife, nonperformance of religious duties, cruelty and incurable disease.[164] In such cases, the wife's financial rights were not compromised. The following cases are examples of court records on *hul* divorce:

"Emine bint Mehmed appointed Veli Efendi as her vekil *(agent) for the matter of* hul *with her husband Haci Abdur-Rahman bn Haci Mustafa. She renounces* mahr *and* nafaka *and receives a* çarşaf *(sheet) and a* yorgan *(quilt) as payment for* hul. *(23 2–3; 13 Şaban 1032)"*

"Sali bn Ali and Mustafa bn Ali testify that Ali bn Ummet told his wife Kamerullah that he divorced her three times if she gave up claim to all payments in money and goods. (22 26–10; 12 Zilhicce 1030)"

"Rabia bint Ali of Gulluck mahalle *acknowledges in the presence of her husband Abdur-Rahman bn Himmet: He gave me half a house in the* mahalle *for* mahr *but since we are not living together ... I gave it back to him, and I renounce claim to* mahr, nafaka, *and other* zevciyyet. *He pronounced* hul *and I accepted some cloth and two kuruş 'bedel-i hul.' Our little daughter Cemile is to stay with me until she is nine. (24 3–5; 28 Cumadi II 1032)"*

Hedayetullah bn Sultan Hoca acknowledges in the presence of his wife Ayna bint Ibadullah who has Abdi Beg as vekil *for the confirmation: We were not living together... When she*

Preziosi, *Women on Promenade*, 1861

renounced claim to mahr, nafaka-i 'iddet, *and other* zevciyyet, *I divorced her* (hul). *I gave certain goods* bedel-i hul. *(27 28–5; 2 Ramadan 1035)*"[165]

Research in Ottoman court records has revealed hundreds of thousands of marriage, divorce and remarriage records. Divorce appears not to have been uncommon. Once the three-month waiting period had elapsed, women were free to remarry and they usually did. Apparently, there was no social stigma placed on either divorcees or widows. Sometimes divorced women remarried their former husbands if three repudiations had not taken place. In such cases a new *mahr* was required and new conditions could be put in a remarriage contract to prevent a repetition of the problem that had initially led to divorce. The following is a case in point:

"When Latifa bint 'Ali ibn Musa agreed to remarry Yahya ibn 'Ubayd ibn 'Ali, she received, in advance, a new dowry of four gold dinars, as well as a commitment that he would pay her five silver nisfs monthly clothing support. In return, she released him from a fourteen-gold-dinar debt to which she had been entitled from their first marriage. As condition for remarrying him, Latifa required that, if he were to take back his other divorced wife at any time, then Latifa would be automatically divorced from him three times, whereby she could never become his wife again, unless she first married and lived with another man (Misr al-Qadima, sijillat 1037/1627, 95:223–1010)."[166]

Polygamy

As has been mentioned, many Ottoman women took precautions against polygamy by stipulating in their marriage and remarriage contracts that they would be divorced if the husband took another wife. Yet, in spite of the fact that polygamy constituted one of the main reasons for divorce,[167] or perhaps due in part to this fact, polygamy was not a widespread phenomenon in Ottoman society. Although legally permitted, polygamy was not socially acceptable in Ottoman society. Many travelers' reports and scholarly researches attest to this. The following are comments regarding polygamy by European travelers:

Turkish woman with veil

M. de M. D'Ohsson:

"Very few Muslims have two wives. It's also very difficult to find rich men with four wives. The difficulty of taking care of them, a concern for domestic peace, the problem of their getting along together and the care parents take in not giving their daughters to married men all prevent polygamy, although it is legally permissible. Many times men can only get a bride with the condition that they won't take another wife as long as they remain married."[168]

Lucy Garnett:

"Notwithstanding the fact that the law of Islam allows a man to marry as many as four wives and to be the owner of an unlimited number of slave women, an Osmanli household is by no means composed—as is popularly supposed in the West—of a large number of women, all of whom stand in wifely relations to their lord and master. Indeed, as a matter of fact, at the present day among Turks of the industrial classes one wife is the rule, and among those of the upper classes more than one wife is the exception. And thus it has, apparently, always more or less been among Moslems generally... Lack of progeny by the first spouse is most frequently the reason of a Turk's incurring this extra expense, and also the risk of having his domestic peace disturbed by taking a second wife... Two wives, indeed, seem to be the extreme limit nowadays; and only once during my long residence in different parts of the Ottoman Empire had I the opportunity of visiting a harem containing even this number. It was during a brief visit made from Smyrna to the ancient and picturesque town of Magnesia—Magnesia under Sipylus—in Asia Minor, and the harem in question was that of the Sheik, or Prior, of the 'Dancing' Dervishes, whose office is, when possible, hereditary. The first wife, to whom he had been married a dozen years or so, was childless, and the 'Ikindji Kadın (second wife) was a bride of a few weeks only."[169]

Anna Bowman Dodd:

"To the casual visitor there is an unexpected embarrassment in finding almost all the Turks one meets, in society, married to one wife. The singularity of this singleness is as trying, apparently, to the Turk on certain occasions, as it is eminently disappointing to the European."[170]

Z. Duckett Ferriman:

"Another erroneous supposition is that polygamy is the rule in Turkey, whereas it is a very rare exception and is becoming rarer every day. The law, it is true, allows four wives, but one may frequent Turkish society a very long time without meeting with an establishment that has more

than one. *To all who are not wealthy, the expense would be a deterrent, for the law requires the husband to provide each wife with a separate suite of apartments, servants, and all the adjuncts of a household—with an establishment of her own, in short. Hence polygamy is an impossibility for the vast majority, whilst among the few who could afford the luxury of a dual establishment monogamy is a matter of preference. Domestic peace is as dear to the Turk as to any one else, and he is pre-eminently a lover of tranquility... The nation is practically monogamist.*"[171]

Lady Montague:

"Turkish women ... are queens of their slaves, whom the husband has no permission so much as to look upon, except it be an old woman or two that his lady chooses. It is true their law permits them four wives; but there is no instance of a man of quality that makes use of this liberty, or of a woman of rank that would suffer it... Amongst all the great men here, I only know the 'tefterdar,' (i.e. treasurer) that keeps a number of she-slaves for his own use (that is, on his own side of the house; for a slave once given to a lady is entirely at her disposal), and he is spoken of as a libertine, or what we should call a rake, and his wife will not see him, though she continues to live in his house."[172]

Scholarly research in court records supports the travelers' opinions that polygamy was very limited in the Ottoman Empire and that when it did occur it was usually because the first wife was barren. This appears to be the only socially acceptable justification for polygamy for the public, although they did not oppose polygamy as an imperial policy of dynastic reproduction.

In the following study of seventeenth century court records in the city of Bursa, only one percent of Ottoman men had more than one wife:

"In the kadıs' *records of seventeenth-century Anatolian Bursa women appear very different than as depicted by the common stereotype. For example, if one examines them in regard to the law curtailing the allowed number of wives to four, a surprising fact emerges. In Bursa it was possible to check this point through extensive lists of estates of people who died in the city during the seventeenth-century. For each of the deceased are supplied various details about the family, such as names of wives and children. From over two thousand estates of males read, it is estimated that in no more than twenty cases did a man have two or more wives. Polygamy evidently existed only in theory, at least in Bursa."*[173]

Other studies made on Bursa show that the above findings were not unique. In sixteenth century court records evidence revealed a polygamy rate of two percent, while another study made on the mid-seventeenth century showed a rate of four percent. A further study made on court records for the years 1839–1876 corroborates these findings with a polygamy rate of two percent.[174]

In a study of Cyprus court records from 1571–1640, Ronald C. Jennings found "very little evidence of polygamy... probably it was uncommon."[175] In his study on Kayseri court records, Jennings mentions a study of estate records (1545–1659) in Edirne made by another scholar who found that ninety-two percent of the married males had one wife, seven percent had two wives, less than one percent had three wives and none had four wives.[176]

Another study made on Istanbul court records from 1885–1906 shows a rate of polygamy of two percent.[177] This is corroborated by a separate study of seventeenth century court records where the rate of monogamy was found to be ninety-two percent. In the ninety-five cases of polygamous marriages, there were 115 children in all, giving an average of 1.2 children per family, which strongly suggests that these men were led to polygamous relationships from a desire to have offspring. In studies made in the Ottoman cities of Istanbul, Edirne, Bursa, Ankara, Damascus and various Anatolian cities, there is only a variance of seven percent, at most, among polygamy rates.[178]

Certainly, the active role of Ottoman women in the courts constituted an important factor in limiting the polygamy rate. Their firm stand on this issue is obvious from the condition many of them put in the wedding contract to the effect that they would be divorced without losing their financial rights if the husband took a second wife and their actually following through with the divorce in cases when he did marry again. There were other deterrents to polygamy, as well, such as those mentioned by European travelers: the high cost of separate quarters for more than one wife, the loss of domestic peace and the refusal of parents to give their daughters to married men.

Yet, polygamy was legal according to the *sharia*. Why did so many Ottoman men refrain from it? One cannot help but wonder if there was not another compelling motive here that led Ottoman men to refrain from polygamy in such great numbers. The law worked as a bottom line in the lives of Ottoman men and women; it told them what they could not do. But they looked to the Qur'an and prophetic traditions in regard to what they should do. On the subject of polygamy the Qur'an permits four wives, but recommends only one.[179] Ensuring justice in all respects to

the women involved is required as a condition of polygamy. Since this is virtually impossible, monogamy is encouraged in order to prevent injustice.

In the life of Prophet Muhammad, peace be upon him, monogamy was clearly the preferred mode of marriage. He lived in a monogamous relationship for twenty-five years with his first wife, Khadija, until her death at age sixty-five. After a year of deep grief and mourning, known as the Year of Sorrow in Islamic history, he married two wives with the encouragement of his Companions. The first, Sawda, was a widow approximately fifty years old. She immediately moved into the Prophet's house where his young daughter Fatima was still living. The second, Aisha, was still a young girl; their marriage was not consummated until three years later. The important point here is that both wives knew about each other and willingly accepted a polygamous relationship from the beginning as, of course, did the wives that followed.

In a situation involving his daughter Fatima, however, the Prophet refused permission for his son-in-law Ali to take another wife. Aware of his daughter's anxiety regarding this matter, Muhammad (peace be upon him), speaking from the pulpit in the masjid in Medina, said:

"The people of Hisham ibn Mughira have asked my permission to marry their daughter to Ali ibn Ali Talib. I do not permit it; again I do not permit it; and again I do not permit it. Of course, if Ali divorces my daughter and marries their daughter, he has the right. My daughter is part of myself. Whatever harms her, harms me; whatever hurts her, hurts me."[180]

Underscoring the pain and harm of polygamy for a woman who is not willing to accept it, the Prophet Muhammad, peace be upon him, stated clearly that Ali's marriage to another woman could only take place after divorce from Fatima. Some scholars say that the reason Fatima did not want this marriage was because the prospective bride was Abu Jahl's daughter rather than that she did not want another wife. However, the fact that Ali did not take any other wife until after Fatima's death supports the view that Fatima did not want any second wife. Regardless of the reason, the Prophet forbid Ali's marrying Abu

Jahl's daughter because it gave harm to his daughter. This example was obviously not lost on Ottoman men and women, because Ottoman women commonly put the stipulation in their marriage contract that they would be automatically divorced without foregoing their *mahr* if their husband took a second wife.

Wife-beating

Although traditional Islamic law which was practiced under the Ottomans permitted light physical chastisement of wives, the conditions under which this was permissible and the degree of chastisement were clearly defined. Firstly, the reason for chastising a woman had to be very serious. The Qur'an mentions disloyalty and ill-conduct on the part of the wife.[181] Secondly, a man could not hit his wife in anger. Initially he had to verbally admonish her. If words had no results, then he could separate their beds. If that brought no results, then he could physically chastise her; however, the chastisement had to be light. A man could not strike his wife on the face or head, and he could not hit her hard enough to make a fracture, wound or bruise. Also, the sayings and conduct of the Prophet Muhammad were one of the major sources of Islamic law and a reference for the courts. The Prophet's wife Aisha stated that the Prophet had never hit any woman or child.

It is clear that women and the wider society were aware of their rights. Although women did not have the right physically to chastise their husbands, they could complain to the *kadı* about such assaults and have their husbands imprisoned or physically chastised as well, depending on the individual case. A case in point was witnessed with amazement by a German tradesman who had been imprisoned for his debts:

"The wives of common men have the right to sue their husbands at court if they do not give their right and cease paying attention to them and fall in love with someone else... Many men who were given to court in this manner

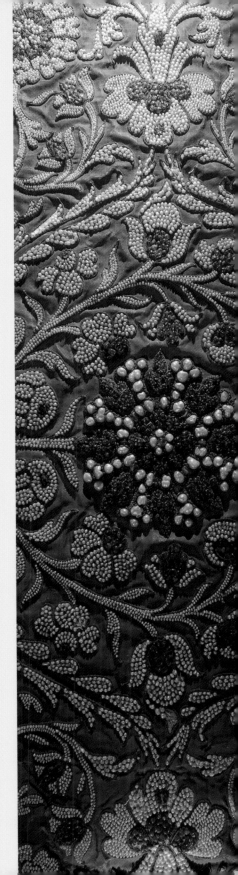

had fallen to our prison. When they entered with anger, aggressiveness and impatience, the other prisoners would give them a sip of water in a wooden ladle and we would welcome them in a ridiculing manner, feeling pity for them. This way that person would cool down and, if he were patient, his situation would improve in a short time. Meanwhile, his friends would try to mediate between the couple. Later on that person would be free with less ridicule and harm in three to four days or in a period longer than that. In a situation like this, particularly we Germans would have beaten the daylights out of her."[182]

Moreover, the husband's hitting his wife more severely than permitted by the *sharia* or hitting her in a place forbidden by the law was a legitimate reason for complaint on the part of the wife, and the court supported the woman if she could prove her case. Husbands could be severely admonished and chastised by the court. The *kadı* usually made the husband accept the condition that if he hit his wife again contrary to the *sharia*, then they would be divorced without the wife forfeiting her financial rights. The following are examples from court records:

"When Imam Nu'man bn Abdul-Vehhab and Osman bn Mehmed and Himmet bn Ali testified that this Abdul-Celil Aga struck his wife, he took an oath that he would not strike her contrary to the sharia. *(23 16-4; 20 Ramadan 1032)"*

"Seydi Ahmed bn Mehmed and Haci Receb Başa bn Mehmed testify that Hasan struck his wife Zahire in a forbidden place today. It was an injustice; it was ruthless. Hasan grants his wife maintenance, admits he struck her contrary to the sharia, *and divorces her. (19 30-11; 28 Rebi II 1026)"*

"Yakub bn Yakub of Alaca Suluk mahalle sets forth a claim in the presence of his wife Safiye bint Hamze: For four months my wife Safiye has not lived with me; she has lived in another place. It is my right to have her with me. Let her be asked. Safiye says Ermenak kadı Ahmed Efendi warned Yakub that if he struck me he would be divorced three times. Yakub accepted this, then he struck me contrary to the sharia, *so I became divorced from him. Yakub denies this. However witnesses former* kadı *Alaeddin Efendi bn Ahmed and Mahmud bn Alaeddin Halife confirm Safiye. They heard Yakub say that Ahmed Efendi had given him this condition. (Karaman 1 8-3; no. 28)"*[183]

Preziosi, *Turkish Woman with her Child*, 1861

Child Custody/Guardianship

Women were usually given custody of their minor children in case of divorce. Boys stayed with their mothers until the age of seven, at which time they could return to their father's household. Girls stayed with their mothers until marriage. The amount of child support was determined by the court and men were legally responsible for paying it. The following is an example:

"The Hanafi qadi gave Amna bint Ibrahim custody of her son, Abu Zayd, following her divorce and estimated a nursing fee of ½ fidda to be paid by her divorcé, the boy's father. Because the latter refused to pay, the judge gave Amna permission to borrow against the money owed her and made the divorcé legally bound to repay it. Amna's custody of Abu Zayd was assumed to last for two years whether she remarried or remained single, lived in town, or moved elsewhere. She was expected back in court after the expiration of the two years, when her custody would be extended, as was usual in such cases. (Tobon, sijillat 1008/1600, 188L57-201)"[184]

When a man died, the court always appointed a legal guardian for his children, which was usually his wife. Although male relatives and other female relatives were sometimes appointed, in the majority of court cases when the mother was living, she was designated as guardian until the child reached adulthood. As guardian, she was responsible for undertaking all kinds of financial transactions regarding the minor child's financial security including protecting the child's property, purchasing property in the child's name, making financial investments, collecting rents and other income and paying off debts. A case in point:

Zonaro, *A Mother's Love*,▲
Dolmabahçe Palace

Wall recess. Twin
Pavilions, Topkapı
Palace ▶

"Mu'mina bint Zayn al-Din 'Abdul-Rahman, the Shaykh of Suq al-Ruba'iyya al-Zahari (i.e., a man of consequence) was made guardian of her minor daughter, Salha, from her deceased husband, Shihab, the merchant 'to look into her (daughter's) affairs and interests and dispose of them by selling, buying, taking and giving, receiving funds or spending, in all legitimate dispositions; and to do what guardians are entitled to do legitimately until the said minor reaches maturity, understands her religious duties, and legitimate handling of money.' (al Qisma al'Arabiyya, sijillat 1035/1626, 57:27-394)"[185]

Inheritance

According to Islamic law, women inherit half the share of men in the same degree of closeness to the deceased. This apparent disparity seems more just when it is remembered that men are fully responsible for the maintenance of women, even in the extended family, which could also include parents, single, divorced, or widowed sisters and aunts, grown daughters, and so on. A woman, on the other hand, is not responsible for her own maintenance and can use her inheritance as she sees fit.

Research to date shows that Ottoman women's inheritance rights were scrupulously upheld by the court. In case of a dispute over an inheritance share, women turned to the court for settlement of the issue, even petitioning the Imperial Council when necessary. The following is such a case:

"Imperial Edict to the Beylerbeyi and kadı of Trabzon and kadıs of Giresun: A man named Süleyman who was domiciled in Giresun was married but since he lived in another place, the wife was allotted support through an official document from the court, however, she died before receiving the support and clothing allowance which was sent. Her daughter who lives in Trabzon, applied to Istanbul and asked for the mahr and support from Süleyman, which was transferred to her according to

▲ A corner of the *hamam*'s cold room, Dolmabahçe Palace

◄ A reception room of the Harem, Dolmabahçe Palace

the sharia *by way of inheritance. He refrained from giving by fabricating excuses, even though the* kadı *sent someone he persisted in not giving it and did not listen to the order of the* sharia. *This has been officially recorded and documented. Thus, I command that the aforementioned Süleyman be brought to Trabzon before the court and the* mahr *and support which he refrains from giving with false excuses must be taken from him and given to the rightful woman's husband, Mustafa, whom she appointed as her power of attorney.* (approx. date 1056 H.)"[186]

Because inheritance was an important source of financial security, Ottoman women were careful to maintain this legal right. After studying Bursa court records, Haim Gerber concluded:

"All these cases clearly show that males in Bursa were not unaware of the possibilities of disinheriting women. But they also show that women's ability to enforce the Islamic law of inheritance was not merely theoretical, but real."[187]

Property Rights

Ottoman women had the right to acquire, control and dispose of their own property as they saw fit, without interference from male relatives including their husbands. Their property and any income from it were solely at their own disposal. No others could sell, rent or use a woman's property without her consent. If they did so, Ottoman women could and did take violators to court. If the property of even a minor girl had been unjustly sold, she could complain to the *kadı* when she reached maturity. If she could prove her case, the property would be returned to her regardless of how many times it had been sold. The following is such a case from Kayseri court records:

"Emine Bint Haci Musa has for vekil *(legal representative) Huseyn bn Huseyn: When my* müvekkile *(charge) was under age, her* nazir *Seydi Ahmed sold houses belonging to her at Sultan Hamami* mahalle *to Haci Hasan. Now she is of age and wants them back. The court orders them to be given to her. (23 48-8, 9; 16 Muharrem 1033 H.)"*[188]

In some cases a parent or parents acted on behalf of their daughter when property had been usurped by the girl's husband:

"In a petition submitted by Banafse on Rebi'l-Awwal 1085/April 1675, she complained that her son-in-law, Halil the Janissary had illegally taken the house and çiftlik *(agricultural estate)*

of her deceased husband, which were inherited by her daughter Fatma, Halil's wife. (Majer 1984, fol. 25a, no.4)"[189]

Women could inherit or purchase property or receive it in the form of *mahr* from their husbands or as a gift. Ottoman women were particularly active in the area of buying, selling and leasing real estate, which provided them with an important source of financial security. In a study made on seventeenth century records of estates in Bursa, a third of the women studied owned houses.[190] The Kayseri court registers show that "the women of Kayseri accumulated an extraordinary proportion of the lands and property in the city." For example, forty percent of 1602 land and property transfers involved at least one woman.[191] In another study made on eighteenth century Aleppo court records, women were involved in sixty-three percent of property sales.[192] Ottoman women's ability to accumulate wealth is corroborated by statistics regarding the establishment of pious foundations. According to registrations in Istanbul in 1546, thirty-six percent of the foundations were established by women.[193] In addition to extensive property ownership that included orchards, gardens and shops as well, Ottoman women also owned farm implements and animals plus household items, clothing, textile goods, jewelry and slaves. They made wide-ranging cash business investments and large formalized loans,[194] all of which attest to the serious financial involvement of women in Ottoman society.

In general, it can be said that Ottoman women made frequent use of the courts and that usually their rights were scrupulously upheld by the courts. In comparison with European women's rights, Ottoman women had a clear edge. Not until 1857 was divorce legalized in Britain, and not until 1936 was there divorce by mutual consent. In 1882 married women were granted property rights; until that time a woman's property went to her husband upon marriage, and she also lost her legal agency as well. In case of separation or divorce, European women could be parted from their children. A good example is Lady Elizabeth Craven who visited the Ottoman Empire in 1786 and wrote a book about her travels. Legally separated from her husband, she had been forcibly separated from her seven children.[195] One European traveler noted in 1903 that the rights of Ottoman women were "so numerous, indeed, that after a review of them, it is the European rather than the Osmanli women who seem to be still in bondage."[196]

Simurg. Illumination by Koç, 2007

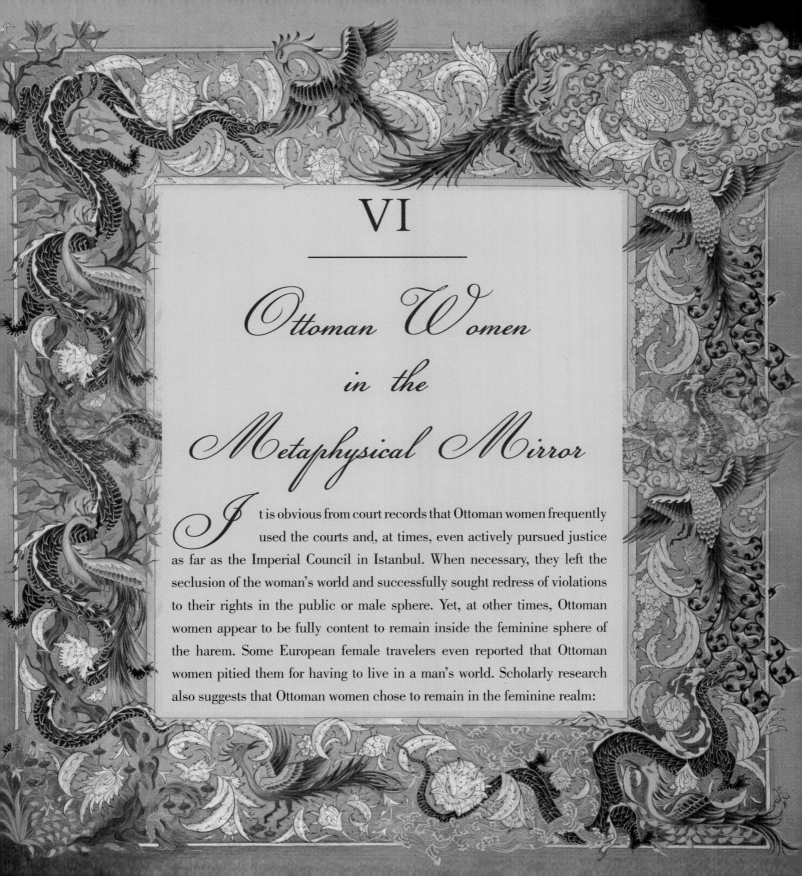

VI

Ottoman Women
in the
Metaphysical Mirror

It is obvious from court records that Ottoman women frequently used the courts and, at times, even actively pursued justice as far as the Imperial Council in Istanbul. When necessary, they left the seclusion of the woman's world and successfully sought redress of violations to their rights in the public or male sphere. Yet, at other times, Ottoman women appear to be fully content to remain inside the feminine sphere of the harem. Some European female travelers even reported that Ottoman women pitied them for having to live in a man's world. Scholarly research also suggests that Ottoman women chose to remain in the feminine realm:

"The evidence available suggests that women of the artisan class as a whole not only accepted their domestic role, but strongly identified with it. At Eskişehir, for instance, the effigies these women chose for their gravestones invariably show them in their preferred household roles—usually surrounded by their children or at work on their looms. Wills deposited at Bursa show a similar identification with the household. This last point is even more succinctly put in the seventeenth-century judicial records of Kayseri, where women divest themselves of extra household property three times more frequently than they acquire it. Thus, women in the Ottoman Empire from the artisan class and above show a marked tendency to eschew the outside world in favor of life within the world of women."[197]

What prompted Ottoman women to identify so completely with the feminine sphere in a society that appears to be strongly patriarchal? Why did they so willingly accept, in fact, choose to live in a sequestered environment basically excluded from the male realm? What was their world paradigm and their *raison d'être*? Of course, there were a number of incentives to attract women to the domestic arena, like financial maintenance, the companionship of a husband and the support of a family network. But beyond these, on the metaphysical plane, there seems to be an even more powerful attraction to the feminine realm for women in Sufi esoteric understanding. According to Harvard professor Cemal Kafadar, *"Scholarly works seem to suggest that affiliation with the [Sufi] orders in the classical and post-classical empire included the entire urban population except for the defenders of the orthodoxy, the religious scholars."*[198] If this was the case, then we can assume that large numbers of Ottoman women were affiliated with Sufi orders and that Sufism had a significant impact on their worldview.

Sufism teaches that men and women are different, but of equal worth. Renowned Muslim scholar and Sufi, Ibn al-Arabi (1165–1240) makes this clear in the following passage:

"Women share with men in all levels, even in being Pole... If the only thing that had reached us concerning this matter were the words of the Prophet, 'Women are the likes of men,' that would be enough, since it means that everything to which a man can attain—stations, levels, or attributes—can also belong to any woman whom God wills, just as it can belong to any man whom God wills."[199]

Sufi doctrine also teaches that God was a Hidden Treasure before the creation of the universe, as is expressed in the following passages from Rumi:

"So God compounded animality and humanity together so that both might be made manifest. 'Things are made clear by their opposites.' It is impossible to make anything known without its opposite. Now God most High possessed no opposite. He says, 'I was a Hidden Treasure, and I wanted to be known.' So He created this world, which is of darkness, in order that His Light might manifest."[200]

"'I was a Hidden Treasure, so I wanted to be known.': 'I was a treasure, concealed behind the curtain of the Unseen, hidden in the retreat of No-place. I wanted My beauty and majesty to be known to see what sort of Water of Life and Alchemy of Happiness I am.'"[201]

Looking at the Sufi understanding that God was a Hidden Treasure before the creation of the universe, it can be understood that the Mercy of the Divine Essence (Hidden Treasure) embraced or surrounded everything before the differentiation and manifestation in the cosmos of the masculine and feminine principles, which were latent in the Divine Essence. This is pointed to in the prophetic tradition that states that God's Mercy precedes His Wrath.[202] Arabi also uses another hadith, "God made me love three things from this world: women, perfume and prayer," to support this idea. He argues that the Prophet Muhammad (peace be upon him) gives precedence to

Calligraphic panel. *Maṣaallah*
"How wonderful what Allah wills."

the feminine over the masculine by putting the masculine noun between two feminine nouns in Arabic grammar.[203]

The elevated position of the feminine is pointed to in the first verse of Sura Nisa (Women) in the Qur'an:

O mankind! Reverence your Guardian-Lord
Who created you from a single Person,
Created, of like nature, his mate,
And from them twain scattered (like seeds)
Countless men and women;
Reverence God through Whom
Ye demand your mutual (rights),
And (reverence) the wombs (that bore you):
For God ever watches over you. (4:1)

In Arabic the word for womb is *rahim*, which means both the uterus where the young are carried and a blood tie or kinship. The sanctity of the womb is indicated by its association with God in this verse: *Reverence God... and the wombs.* Moreover, the birth of a child can be associated with the creation of the universe. One is the birth of a microcosm in human form and the other is the birth of the macrocosm. Of course, the association can also be made between the female womb and the Hidden Treasure, which is implied in the following hadith:

"God said, 'I am God and I am the All-Merciful. I created the womb and I gave it a name derived from My own name [ar-Rahim]. Hence if someone cuts off the womb, I will cut him off, but if someone joins the womb, I will join him to Me.'"[204]

The degree to which Ottoman men gave reverence to the wombs that bore them can be seen, for example, in the sultans' treatment of their mothers, the *valide sultans*. The queen mother was the only person in the whole Empire to whom the sultan showed public deference. Similarly, in the society at large, mothers were always treated with utmost respect and honor. Respect for the feminine was generally extended to all other females entrusted to a man, that is, his wife, daughters, other female relatives and female slaves who were protected and cared for in the harem. Some men even bought elderly or crippled female slaves and took care of them in the harem simply to gain God's favor. In view of this, it is not difficult to understand why Ottoman women identified with the feminine world and willingly chose to be a part of it. Rather than seeing the harem or feminine world as a sphere of confinement and oppression, Ottoman women saw it as a place where they were honored and protected as females, in accordance with the cosmic hierarchy. It is important to note that there was not a strict male-female dichotomy in the Ottoman harem. Rather, there was an elder-younger dichotomy in which the husband's mother took precedence, followed by her son, then his wife, and then the younger members of the family in order of their birth. The elder child, regardless of whether it was a boy or girl, always had authority over the younger child and carried responsibilities towards it. The younger child was expected to respect and obey that authority.

Another important point of Sufi teaching is balance in the microcosm, or a person's inner world, which is a reflection of the macrocosm or universe. According to Sufism, all of creation is, in fact, a manifestation of God's attributes, as in indicated in the following quote from Rumi:

"God says, 'I was a Hidden Treasure, so I wanted to be known.' In other words, 'I created the whole of the universe, and the goal of all of it is to make Myself manifest,

Lewis, *Harem*, 1838

Wilkie, *Mrs. Young*, 1843

sometimes through gentleness and sometimes through severity.' God is not the kind of king for whom a single herald would be sufficient. If all the atoms of the universe were His heralds, they would be incapable of making Him known adequately."[205]

Limited human beings can never fully know God, but they can know Him by His names or attributes. According to Sachiko Murata, a well-known scholar on Islam, God's names can be generally categorized in terms of Incomparability (*tanzih*) and Similarity (*tashbih*) or the names of Majesty (*Jalal*) and Beauty (*Jamal*).[206] All the names are latent in all human beings, but Murata argues that the names of Majesty, which reflect qualities like majesty, power and justice, reflect the cosmic male principle; whereas the names of Beauty, which reflect qualities like love, forgiveness, gentleness and compassion, reflect the cosmic female principle. Consequently, the names of Majesty are usually more apparent in males, while the names of Beauty are usually more apparent in females. According to Sufi doctrine, regardless of which names are more apparent in a human being, it is the purpose of each person to bring the divine names or attributes, which all exist in a person's inner world, into perfect balance and harmony so that no name dominates another.[207]

The person who has successfully brought the divine names into balance in his/her inner world has become the *insan-ı kâmil* or perfected human being. In general, women naturally tend to manifest *Jamal* or feminine attributes like beauty, receptivity, kindness, forgiveness, and compassion. It is their challenge, then, to strengthen their *Jalal* or masculine attributes like courage and bravery in the active pursuit of justice. Men, on the other hand, usually manifest *Jalal* or masculine characteristics like assertiveness and ambition; it is their challenge to cultivate *Jamal* attributes like patience and humility. If all the divine attributes can be brought into

Tombstone of Turkish woman. Eyüp, Istanbul ▶

balance in a person's inner world, then the person reflects the Divine. The balanced person becomes a metaphysical mirror in which God can see Himself.

To what degree did Ottoman women attain balance in their inner world? Of course, there are no historical documents or travelers' reports that can directly address this issue. However, a conclusion can be derived by looking at the evidence at hand. It has already been seen from the descriptions of Europeans who met them that Ottoman women were extremely feminine in appearance and behavior. Also they strongly identified with their domestic roles as wife and mother. Moreover, they obviously found fulfillment in life within the harem and the larger social world of women. On the other hand, they showed extreme courage and determination when their rights had been violated. In view of travel conditions of the day, it is amazing that women from distant parts of the empire pursued their quest for justice all the way to the Imperial Court in Istanbul. It is clear that women of all ages and social strata dared to challenge in the legal arena their close male relatives like husbands, fathers and uncles. In view of this, it appears safe to conclude that many Ottoman women were remarkably balanced human beings, who generally manifested the attributes of Beauty but who could respond to injustice with the attributes of Majesty, when necessary. Perhaps this is the Ottoman woman's greatest legacy to humanity.

Calligraphic panel. Arabic letter *wav* ▶

◀ Illumination detail by Koç, 2007

Acknowledgments

My deep gratitude goes to my daughter Selime, who has been my constant companion on this journey of discovery in the Ottoman woman's world; to my son Şahin, who has given hands-on support throughout the publishing process, particularly with the art design; and to my son Mustafa, who has offered encouragement and moral support throughout the project. Also, my sincere appreciation goes to the whole staff at The Light, Inc. publishing company. In particular, to Fikret Yaşar for supporting this project; to Hakan Yeşilova for his sincere effort every step of the way and for his openness to new ideas; and to Engin Çiftçi and the whole art department, especially İhsan Demirhan and İbrahim Akdağ who illustrated the spirit of the book so well.

Picture Credits

PAGE 2: Textile detail from Audience Chamber, Topkapı Palace Museum.

PAGE 6–7, 42–43, 48–49, 54–55, 56–57: Embedded detail from Karamemi's decoration of flowers in Kanuni's *Divan*. Kanuni wrote with the pen name Muhibbi. *Muhibbi Divanı*, Istanbul University Library, T5467.

PAGE 6: Osman Hamdi, *Girl Picking Lilacs* (private collection).

PAGE 8: Fausto Zonaro, *Amusement at Göksu*, (after 1910). Oil on canvas. Suna and İnan Kıraç Collection.

PAGE 10: (Left) Abdullah Frères, *Turkish woman*, 1880s. Abdul-Hamid II Collection (Library of Congress). (Below right) Covered cup. 1902. Dolmabahçe Palace Museum, Objets de Vertu Exhibition II, 37/943.

PAGE 11 and 12: Coffee table and woman (cropped from) Jean-Etienne Liotard's (1702–89) *Monsieur Levett and Mademoiselle Helene Glavany in Turkish Costumes*. Oil on canvas. ©Louvre, Paris, France/ Giraudon/ The Bridgeman Art Library.

PAGE 15: Jean-Baptiste Hilair, *Ladies of the harem taking a collation under a pavilion*, 1798(?). Watercolor and gouache. Musée de Louvre, Paris. Inv. R.F. 26958.

PAGE 16: (Painter unknown), *Young Woman*, 18th century. Oil on metal. Suna and İnan Kıraç Foundation Collection.

PAGE 18: Osman Hamdi, *From Harem* (detail), 1880.

PAGE 19: Mirror. 16th century. Topkapı Palace Museum 2/1797.

PAGE 21: Marquis de Ferriol, *Woman Working Embroidery*. Recueil de Cent Estampes Représentant Différentes Nations du Levant, Paris 1714. Copper plate. Galeri Alfa slide archive.

PAGE 22: Detail from a *sitil puşide*, a cover used while serving coffee in a cup. Dolmabahçe Palace Museum, 39/156.

PAGE 24: The Sultan's hamam in the harem, Topkapı Palace. Photo Mustafa Yılmaz.

PAGE 24–25: Tap made of copper. Topkapı Palace Museum. Harem.

PAGE 25: Clogs made of wood and silver. Topkapı Palace Museum, Silver Section 16/2098.

PAGE 26: Prayer beads. Privy Chamber (Has Oda), Topkapı Palace Museum 21/264.

PAGE 26–27: (Embedded) Calligraphy, *"Huwal Baqi."* Topkapı Palace Museum EH 2012.

PAGE 29: Camille Rogier, *Eating in the Harem*, La Turquie. Moeurs et Usages des Orientaux au XIX siecle, London 1848. Lithograph on color sepia. Galeri Alfa, slide archive.

PAGE 30: Flower. Ali Üsküdarî İÜK., T5650 26b.

PAGE 31: Jean Brindesi, *Ladies at the Küçüksu Fountain*, 1850s. Souvenirs de Constantinople. Paris 1855–60. Colored lithograph. Galeri Alfa slide archive. (Below left) Silver coffee pot, 19th century. Topkapı Palace Museum 2/1914.

PAGE 34: Camille Rogier, *Drapers in the Covered Bazaar*, La Turquie. Moeurs et Usages des Orientaux au XIX siecle. London, 1848. Lithograph on color sepia.

PAGE 36: Ottoman house interior. Çamlıca, Istanbul. Photo courtesy of Hasan Hayri Demirel.

PAGE 37. Osman Hamdi, *Dressing Up*. Dolmabahçe Palace Museum.

PAGE 39: John Frederick Lewis, *The Reception*, 1873. Oil on panel. ©Yale Center for British Art, Paul Mellon Collection, USA/The Bridgeman Art Library.

PAGE 41: Van Loo, *Eunuchs Serving the Sultan*, 1772–1773. Nice, Musée Cheret.

PAGE 44–45: Yazdani, The Ka'ba, Mecca, 2006. Kaynak Publishing Group archive.

PAGE 45: Calligraphic panel, 1849: "Allah, may His Glory be exalted; Muhammad, peace be upon him." Museum of Turkish and Islamic Arts, 2780.

PAGE 46: Ottoman house on the Bosphorous. Photo courtesy of Greg Barton.

PAGE 47: (Above) Hercule Catenacci, *Amcazade Hüseyin Paşa Yalısı (Köprülü) Divanhanesi*, Tour du Monde, 1863. Original woodprint. Ayşe Yetişkin Kubilay archive. (Below right) Incense burner, 1885, Topkapı Palace Museum 2/3374.

PAGE 48: Twin Pavilions, Topkapı Palace Museum. Photo Mustafa Yılmaz.

PAGE 49: (Far right) Curtain. Prophyry Room. Dolmabahçe Palace Museum. (Right) Flower decoration on the margin of *Elifba cüzü*. Topkapı Palace Museum, EH436, 17b.

PAGE 50: Amadeo Preziosi, *Spice-seller*, Stamboul. Souvenir d'Orient, Paris, 1861. Colored lithograph.

PAGE 51: Amadeo Preziosi, *Confectioner*, Stamboul. Souvenir d'Orient, Paris, 1861. Colored lithograph.

PAGE 52: John Frederick Lewis, *Entrance to the Harem*, 1871. Oil on board. ©Cecil Higgins Art Gallery, Bedford, Bedfordshire, UK/The Bridgeman Art Library.

PAGE 56: John Frederick Lewis, *School*, London. c. 1850. Steelprint. Galeri Alfa slide archive.

PAGE 57: (Above) Abdullah Frères, *Middle school for girls Sultan Ahmed Inas Rusdiyesi*, between 1880 and 1893. Abdul-Hamid II Collection (Library of Congress). (below right) Abdullah Frères, *Students, private school Darüt-Tahsil*, between 1880 and 1893. Abdul-Hamid II Collection (Library of Congress).

PAGE 58–73, 124–125: Flowers (embedded). Ali Üsküdarî İÜK., T5650 26b.

PAGE 60: Camille Rogier, *Halayik Serving Coffee*, La Turquie. Moeurs et Usages des Orientaux au XIX siecle, London, 1848. Lithograph on color sepia. Galeri Alfa slide archive.

PAGE 62: Amadeo Preziosi, *Caique*, Stamboul. Souvenir d'Orient, Paris, 1858. Colored lithograph. Galeri Alfa slide archive. (Embedded) Parade shield, 16th century. Topkapı Palace Museum, 1/2571.

PAGE 67: A. I. Melling, *Turkish Wedding Parade*. This work first appeared in Melling's *Voyage Pittoresque de Constantinople et des Rives du Bosphore* (Paris, 1819) album. The lithograph was published in J. Goubaud's work in 1840 (Brussels). Original lithograph. Ayşe Yetişkin Kubilay archive.

PAGE 68: Cornelius Le Bruyn, *Women's Turbans*, Voyage au Levant. Paris, 1700. Copperprint. Galeri Alfa slide archive.

PAGE 69: *Şerbet mahraması*. Fruit drink kerchief. Dolmabahçe Palace Museum 40/148.

PAGE 73: Birthing chair. 18–19th century. Topkapı Palace Museum 12/175.

PAGE 75: Cradle. Topkapı Palace Museum, H2/680.

PAGE 76: A. I. Melling, *Hatice Sultan Palace*, interior. 19th century. Defterdarburnu. Topkapı Palace Museum, Y.B. 3441 Vol. III.

PAGE 77: Wall decoration. Fruit Room, Topkapı Palace Museum. Photo Mustafa Yılmaz.

PAGE 81: Tristam (Tristram) James Ellis, *Excursion on the Golden Horn*, 1888. Watercolor and tempera on cardboard. Suna and İnan Kıraç Foundation Collection.

PAGE 82: Bowl. Silver. 19th century. Topkapı Palace Museum 16/1152.

PAGE 83: Jean-Etienne Liotard, *Turkish Woman with her Slave*. 18th century. Pastel on paper. ©Musee d'Art et d'Histoire, Geneva, Switzerland/ Giraudon/ The Bridgeman Art Library.

PAGE 86: Camille Rogier, *Washing Hands in the Harem*, La Turquie. Moeurs et Usages des Orientaux au XIX siecle, London 1848. Lithograph on color sepia.

PAGE 87: Ewer and basin. 18th century. Topkapı Palace Museum 25/3731 and 25/3730.

PAGE 88: Jean-Etienne Liotard, *Portrait of Maria Adelaide (1732–1800) of France in Turkish Costume*, 1753. Oil on canvas. ©Galleria degli Uffizi, Florence, Italy/The Bridgeman Art Library.

PAGE 91: Osman Hamdi, *Two Musician Girls*, 1880. Oil on canvas. Suna and İnan Kıraç Foundation Collection.

PAGE 95: Pascal Sébah, Ayşe Sultan, daughter of Abdülhamid II, with her mother Müşfika Hanımefendi.

PAGE 96: Flower. Ali Üsküdarî İÜK., T5650 41a.

PAGE 97: John Frederick Lewis, *In the Bey's Garden*, 1865. Panel. © Harris Museum and Art Gallery, Preston, Lancashire, UK/ The Bridgeman Art Library.

PAGE 98: Jeweled cup, 16th century. Topkapı Palace Museum 15/2816.

PAGE 99: Unknown painter (French School), *Enjoying Coffee*, 18th century (first half). Oil on canvas. Suna and İnan Kıraç Foundation Collection.

PAGE 100: Jean-Baptiste Hilair, *Ladies of the harem taking a walk*, 1797. Watercolor and gouache. Musée de Louvre, Paris. Inv. R.F. 26659.

PAGE 101. Illumination. Topkapı Palace Museum, EH 416.

PAGE 102: Wall recess. Sultan Ahmed I Privy Chamber, Topkapı Palace Museum. Photo Mustafa Yılmaz.

PAGE 103: Twin Pavilions, Topkapı Palace. Photo Mustafa Yılmaz.

PAGE 106–107: Cornelius Loos, *Topkapı Palace and some seaside mansions*, 1710. The Museum of Fine Arts, Stockholm, THC9116.

PAGE 107: Alberto Pasini, *A Corner of the Harem*, 1877. (below right) Ali Üsküdarî İÜK., T5650 90a.

PAGE 112: Mihrişah Sultan Fountain, 1801. Eyüp, Istanbul. Photo courtesy of Talha Uğurluel.

PAGE 112–113: Flowers. *Kur'an ve Risaleler* (The Qur'an and Epistles) 1757–8. Topkapı Palace Museum EH 141, 444a.

PAGE 114: Pertevniyal Valide Mosque, 1871. Aksaray, Istanbul. Photo courtesy of Talha Uğurluel.

PAGE 115: Mığırdıç Melkon, *Beşiktaş Palace*, Istanbul Naval Museum. Embossed painting.

PAGE 116: Mirror detail. Topkapı Palace Museum, H1795.

PAGE 117: Rosewater flask. Topkapı Palace Museum, H2/2875.

PAGE 118: Osman III Kiosk, Topkapı Palace Museum. Photo Mustafa Yılmaz.

PAGE 118: Jewel detail. Topkapı Palace Museum, H2/1653.

PAGE 119: Lady's dress (*üçetek entari*). Dolmabahçe Palace Museum 64/1973.

PAGE 122: *Şakayık* (peony). Murakka, Topkapı Palace Museum, H2155, 39b.

PAGE 123: Backround detail of an Ottoman *caftan*. Mirror detail (around Hürrem Sultan's portrait). Topkapı Palace Museum, H2/1805.

PAGE 126: Bowl. 18th century. Topkapı Palace Museum, 25/3483.

PAGE 127: Mehmet IV Pavilion, Topkapı Palace Museum. Photo Mustafa Yılmaz.

PAGE 130: Jewelry chest. Dolmabahçe Palace Museum.

PAGE 131: Levni, Turkish woman miniature. Topkapı Palace Museum, Murakka, H2164.

PAGE 132: Fountain. Hall with a Fountain (Çeşmeli Sofa), Topkapı Palace Museum. Photo Mustafa Yılmaz.

PAGE 133: Mirror detail. Topkapı Palace Museum, H2/1786.

PAGE 134: Levni, Turkish woman miniature. Topkapı Palace Museum, Murakka, H2164.

PAGE 135: The Favorites' Courtyard. Topkapı Palace Museum. Photo Mustafa Yılmaz.

PAGE 136: Thomas Allom, *The Petition Writer* (*arzuhalci*), 1840.

PAGE 138: Topkapı Palace. Photo Halit Ömer Camcı.

PAGE 140: Pendant. Topkapı Palace Museum, H 2/7622.

PAGE 141: Ernst Rietschel, *Petition Writers*, 1855–60. Original watercolor. Galeri Alfa slide archive.

PAGE 145: Jean Brindesi, *Passenger Boat in front of the Rumeli Fortress*. Souvenirs de Constantinople. Paris 1855–60. Colored lithograph. Galeri Alfa slide archive.

PAGE 147: The Holy Qur'an cover. Topkapı Palace Museum, H2/2107.

PAGE 149: Amadeo Preziosi, *Women on Promenade*, Stamboul. Souvenir d'Orient, Paris 1861. Colored lithograph. Galeri Alfa slide archive.

PAGE 150: *Turkish woman with veil*. Topkapı Palace Museum, H2164, y.14b.

PAGE 154–155: Flagpole (*alem*). Topkapı Palace Museum. Textile (detail). Topkapı Palace Museum. Photo Mustafa Yılmaz.

PAGE 157: Amadeo Preziosi, *Turkish Woman with her Child*, Stamboul. Souvenir d'Orient, Paris 1861. Colored lithograph.

PAGE 158: Fausto Zonaro, *A Mother's Love*. Dolmabahçe Palace Museum.

PAGE 160–161: The reception room of the Harem. A corner of the *hamam*'s cold room, Dolmabahçe Palace.

PAGE 164 and 165: Simurg. Illumination by Ayşe Koç, 2007.

PAGE 166–167: Detail from the arm of a *caftan*. Topkapı Palace Museum 13/933.

PAGE 168: *Maşaallah* and the *nazar* verse (Qalam 68:51–2). Illumination by Ayşe Koç. Calligraphy by Erol Dönmez (Abdülhadi).

PAGE 169: John F. Lewis, *Harem*, Lewis' Illustrations of Constantinople, London, 1838. Lithograph on color sepia. Galeri Alfa slide archive.

PAGE 170: Sir David Wilkie, *Mrs. Young*. Original steel print produced after Sir David Wilkie's Sketches in Turkey, Syria&Egypt in 1840 and 1841 album. London, 1843. Ayşe Yetişkin Kubilay archive.

PAGE 171: Tombstone of a Turkish woman. Eyüp, Istanbul. Photo courtesy of Talha Uğurluel.

PAGE 172: Illumination by Ayşe Koç, 2007.

PAGE 173: Arabic letter "*wav*." Ulu Cami, Bursa.

PAGE 192: Textile detail from Audience Chamber, Topkapı Palace Museum.

Notes

1   Z. Duckett Ferriman, *Turkey and the Turks*, (New York: James Pott & Co., 1911), 84–85.

2   Lady Mary Wortley Montague, *Letters from the Levant during the Embassy to Constantinople 1716–18*, reprint edition (New York: Arno Press & The New York Times, 1971), 154.

3   Ibid., 188.

4   Ibid., ix.

5   Miss Julia Pardoe, *The City of the Sultan and Domestic Manners of the Turks in 1836*, 3 volumes (London: Henry Colburn, 1938), 130.

6   Ibid., 82–84.

7   Ibid., 85.

8   Ibid., 102–3.

9   Lady W. M. Ramsey, *Everyday Life in Turkey* (London: Hodder and Stoughton, 1897), 1.

10 Ferriman, 339–40.

11 Pardoe, Vol. II, 86.

12 Ramsey, 39.

13 Montague, 126.

14 Ibid., 160–61.

15 M. De M. D'Ohsson, *18. Yüzyıl Türkiye'sinde Örf ve Adetler* (Istanbul: Kervan Kitapçılık), 99–102.

16 Pardoe, Vol. III, 85–6.

17 Ferriman, 73.

18 D'Ohsson, 204.

19 Lucy M. Garnett, *Home Life In Turkey* (New York: The MacMillan Company, 1909) 6–7.

20 Mary Adelaid Walker, *Eastern Life and Scenery, with Excursions in Asia Minor, Mytilene, Crete and Roumania.* (London: Chapman and Hall, 1886,) 315–316.

21 Pardoe, 52–53.

22 Ibid., Vol. III, 40.

23 Ibid., 87–88.

24 D'Ohsson, 186–187.

25 Pardoe, Vol. III, 46.

26 Ibid., 58.

27 D'Ohsson, 195.

28 Ibid., 209.

29 Ibid., 208.

30 La Baronne Durand de Fontmagne, *Kırım Harbi Sonrasında Istanbul (Istanbul After the Crimean War)*, (Paris: 1902), 243–44.

31 Montague, 128.

32 Pardoe, Vol. I, 96–97.

33 Ferriman, 317–18.

34 Garnett, 1.

35 Pardoe, Vol III, 94–95.

36 Edmondo de Amicus, *Constantinople* (Paris: 1883), 210.

37 Fontmagne, 243.

38 A. L. Castellan, *Lettres Sur la Grece, L'Hellespont et Constantinople*, Vol III, (1811), 226.

39 Lady Craven, *Voyage de Millady Craven and Constantinople Per la Crimee en 1786*, (Paris: 1789), 253.

40 D'Ohsson, 221.

41 Elizabeth Cooper, *The Harim and Purdah* (New York: The Century Co., 1916), 33–34.

42 Judy Mabro, *Veiled Half-Truths: Western travellers' perceptions of Middle Eastern women* (London: 1991), 9.

43 Montague, 189.

44 Ibid., 202.

45 Catherine Elwood, *Narrative of a Journey Overland*, Vol. I, pp. 153–4 quoted from Billie Melman, *Women's Orients: English Women and the Middle East, 1718–1918 / Sexuality, Religion and Work* (London: Macmillan Academic and Professional Ltd., 1992), 139.

46 Leslie Peirce, *The Imperial Harem / Women and Sovereignty in the Ottoman Empire* (New York – Oxford: Oxford University Press, 1993), 4.

47 Ibid., 5.

48 Ferriman, 80.

49 Montague, 152–54.

50 Lucy Garnett, *Turkey of the Ottomans* (New York, 1914), 203–5.

51 Ibid., 264–65.

52 Emine Fuat Tugay, *Three Centuries, Family Chronicles of Turkey and Egypt* (London – New York – Toronto: 1963), 255.

53 Tugay, ibid., 251.

54 *The Holy Quran / Translation and Commentary* by A. Yusuf Ali (Washington D.C.: The American International Printing Company, 1946), 178.

55 Ferriman, 89.

56 Garnett, 267.

57 Cemal Kutay, *Pembe Mendil* (Istanbul: Yeni Asya Yayınevi), 65–67.

58 De Fontmagne, 243–44.

59 Castellan, 226.

60 Ramsey, 109–10.

61 Pardoe, Vol. I, 93.

62 Kutay, 37.

63 Münevver Ayaşlı, personal interview with author, Istanbul, 1988.

64 Ömer Seyfettin, *Bahar ve Kelebekler* (Istanbul: Inkilap ve AKA Basımevi, 1981), 10–13.

65 Fanny Davis, *The Ottoman Lady/A Social History from 1718 to 1918* (Westport: Greenwood Press, Inc., 1986), 66.

66 Ibid., 69.

67 Garnett, *Home Life in Turkey*, 243.

68 Ibid., 244–45.

69 Melek Hanım, *Thirty Years in the Harem* (London: Chapman and Hall, 1872), 249–50.

70 Pardoe, Vol. II, 96–105.

71 Garnett, 232–33.

72 Ibid., 252–53.

73 Ibid., 146–47.

74 Pardoe, Vol. I, 125–26.

75 Ibid., Vol. III, 83–84.

76 Tugay, 226–27.

77 Pardoe, Vol. I, 98–99.

78 Melman, 147.

79 Ibid., 146.

80 Pardoe, Vol. I, 99.

81 Davis, 113–14.

82 Ferriman, 116–17.

83 Tugay, 220.

84 Leyla Saz, *The Imperial Harem of the Sultans/Memoirs of Leyla (Saz) Hanımefendi*, (Istanbul: Peva Publications, 1994), 66–67.

85 Ibid., 67.

86 Melman, 148.

87 Tugay, 305.

88 Pardoe, 286–87.

89 Çağatay Uluçay, *Harem*, 2nd ed. (Ankara: Türk Tarih Kurumu Basımevi, 1985), 25–26.

90 Peirce, 30.

91 Ibid., 109.

92 Ahmed Akgündüz, *Osmanlı'da Harem*, (Istanbul: Osmanlı Araştırmaları Vakfı, 1995), 277.

93 Ibid., 113.

94 Ibid., 140.

95 Uluçay, 19.

96 Peirce, 235.

97 Akgündüz, 276.

98 Davis, 10.

99 Uluçay, 64–65.

100 Peirce, 252.

101 Ibid., 189.

102 Ibid., 126.

103 Uluçay, 16.

104 Ibid., 162.

105 Peirce, 193.

106 Ibid., 195.

107 Foundation for Establishing and Developing Historical Research and Documentation Centers, *Deeds of Trust of the Sultans' Womenfolk* (Istanbul: 1990), 535.

108 Peirce, 215–16.

109 Ibid., 199.

110 Nimet Bayraktar, "Tarihte Hayırsever Türk Kadınları: Nurbanu Sultan – Kütüphanesi," *Kadın Gazetesi*, No. 541, (Jan. 15, 1959).

111 Bayraktar, "Tarihte Hayırsever Türk Kadınları: Mahpeyker Sultan (Kösem Valide) ve Çinili Cami," *Kadın Gazetesi*, No. 553 (April 11, 1959).

112 Foundation for Establishing and Developing Historical Research and Documentation Centers, 62.

113 Çağatay Uluçay, *Padişahların Kadınları ve Kızları* (Ankara: Türk Tarih Kurumu Basımevi, 1985), 68.

114 Foundation for Establishing and Developing Historical Research and Documentation Centers, 92.

115 Uluçay, *Padişahların Kadınları ve Kızları*, 99.

116 Bayraktar, "Tarihte Hayırsever Türk Kadınları: Nakşidil Valide Sultan," *Kadın Gazetesi*, No. 560 (May 30, 1959).

117 Foundation for Establishing and Developing Historical Research and Documentation Centers, 392.

118 See Bezm-i Alem Valide Sultan Vakıf Gureba Hospital catalogue (Istanbul: 1987).

119 Bayraktar, "Tarihte Hayırsever Türk Kadınları: Pertevniyal Sultan ve Kütüphanesi," *Kadın Gazetesi*, No. 549 (March 14, 1959).

120 Akgündüz, 314.

121 Çağatay, *Harem*, 59–60.

122 Akgündüz, 329.

123 Çağatay, *Harem*, 59.

124 Peirce, 129.

125 Çağatay, *Harem*, 54.

126 Ibid., 53.

127 Montague, 124–25.

128 Saz, 29.

129 Ibid., 102.

130 Ibid., 36–37.

131 Ibid., 111–13.

132 Ibid., 138.

133 Peirce, 200.

134 Çağatay, *Harem*, 70–77.

135 Ibid., 78–81.

136 Ayşe Osmanoğlu, *Babam Sultan Abdülhamid (Hatıralarım)*, (Ankara: Selçuk Yayınları, 1986), 117–18.

137 Saz, 102.

138 Ibid., 138.

139 Peirce, 130.

140 Saz, 115.

141 Çağlar, *Harem*, 100–108.

142 Bayraktar, "Tarihte Hayırsever Türk Kadınları: Mihrimah Sultan ve Camiler," *Kadın Gazetesi*, No. 551, (March 28, 1959).

143 Bayraktar, "Tarihte Hayırsever Türk Kadınları: İsmihan Sultan ve Kütüphanesi," *Kadın Gazetesi*, No. 542, (January 24, 1959).

144 Bayraktar, "Tarihte Hayırsever Türk Kadınları: Zeyneb Sultan ve Camii," *Kadın Gazetesi*, No. 559, (May 23, 1959).

145 Çağlar, *Harem*, 139.

146 Peirce, 132.

147 Çağlar, *Harem*, 132–40

148 Peirce, 133.

149 Ibid., 134.

150 Saz, 128.

151 Garnett, 282–83.

152 Fariba Zarinebaf-Shahr, "Women, Law and Imperial Justice in Ottoman Istanbul in the Late Seventeenth Century," in *Women, the Family, and Divorce Laws in Islamic History*, edited by Madeline C. Zilfi, (Leiden-New York-Köln: Brill, 1997), 255–56.

153 Yvonne Seng, *The Üsküdar Estates (Tereke) as Records of Everyday Life in an Ottoman Town, 1521–1524* (Ph.D. dissertation, University of Chicago, 1991), 230.

154 Ronald C. Jennings, *Christians and Muslims in Ottoman Cyprus and the Mediterranean World, 1571–1640*, (New York and London: New York University Press, 1993), 75.

155 Haim Gerber, *State, Society, and Law in Islam/Ottoman Law in Comparative Study*, (Albany: State University of New York Press, 1994), 56.

156 Jennings, "Women in Early 17th Century Ottoman Judicial Records – The Sharia Court of Anatolian Kayseri," *Journal of the Economic and Social History of the Orient 18*, (January 1975), 78.

157 Ibid., 77.

158 Abdal-Rehim Abdal-Rahman Abdal-Rehim, "The Family and Gender Laws in Egypt During the Ottoman Period," in *Women, the Family and Divorce Laws in Islamic History*, ed. Amira Al Azhary Sonbul, (Syracuse, New York: Syracuse University Press, 1996), 99.

159 Abdurrahman Kurt, "Tanzimat Döneminde Kadının Sosyo-Ekonomik Konumu, Bursa Örneği (1839–1876), unpublished paper, 11.

160 Abdal-Rehim, 99.

161 Kurt, 11.

162 Jennings, "Women in Early 17th Century Ottoman Judicial Records / The Sharia Court of Anatolian Kayseri," 62.

163 Rifat Özdemir, "Kırşehir'de Ailenin Sosyo-Ekonomik Yapısı," *The Journal of Ottoman Studies, Vol. IX,* (Istanbul: Enderun Kitapevi, 1989), 120.

164 The different schools of law accepted different grounds for *hul* divorce. For discussion of these, see Galal H. el-Nahal, *Judicial Administration of Ottoman Egypt in the 17th Century,* (Minneapolis: Bibliotheca Islamica, 1979), 46–47.

165 Jennings, "Women In Early 17th Century Ottoman Judicial Records / The Sharia Court of Anatolian Kayseri," 83.

166 Abdal-Rahim, 107.

167 Ibid., 107.

168 D'Ohsson, 206.

169 Garnett, 220–21.

170 Anna Bowman Dodd, quoted from Melman, 142.

171 Ferriman, 83–84.

172 Montegu, 128–29.

173 Gerber, "Social and Economic Position of Women in an Ottoman City, Bursa, 1600–1700," *International Journal of Middle East Studies, 12,* (Cambridge: Cambridge University Press, 1980), 232.

174 Kurt, 13–14.

175 Jennings, *Christians and Muslims in Ottoman Cyprus and the Mediterranean World, 1571–1640,* 29.

176 Jennings, "Women In Early 17th Century Ottoman Judicial Records / The Sharia Court of Anatolian Kayseri," 98.

177 Cem Behar, "Polygyny in Istanbul 1889–1926," *Middle Eastern Studies,* vol. 27/3, July 1991, 477–78.

178 Said Öztürk, "Osmanlı Ailesi Üzerine Düşünceler," *İlim ve Sanat* Magazine, vols. 44–45, (Istanbul: Vefa Yayıncılık, 1997), 63.

179 See Quran 4/3: "If you believe that ye shall not be able to deal justly with the orphans, marry women of your choice, two, or three, or four; but if ye fear that ye shall not be able to deal justly (with them), then only one, or (a captive) that your right hands possess. That will be more suitable to prevent you from doing injustice." 4/129: "You are never able to be fair and just as between women, even if it is your ardent desire." *The Holy Qur'an/Text, Translation and Commentary* by Abdullah Yusuf Ali. (Washington D.C.:The American International Printing Company, 1946), 179, 221.

180 Sahih Bukhari, *Kitab un-nikah.*

181 See Quran 4/34: As to those women on whose part ye fear disloyalty and ill-conduct, admonish them (first), (next) refuse to share their beds, (and last) beat them (lightly); but if they return to obedience, seek not against them means (of annoyance).

182 H. U. Krafft, *Türklerin Elinde Bir Alman Tacir - Ein Schwabischer Kaufman in Türkischer Gefangenschaftö* trans. by Turgut Akpınar, (Istanbul: İletişim, 1996), 54–55.

183 Jennings, *Women in Early 17th Century Ottoman Judicial Records / The Sharia Court of Anatolian Kayseri,* 92.

184 Abdal-Rahim, 108–09.

185 Ibid., 109.

186 *Mühimme Defteri 90,* ed. Mertol Tulum (Istanbul: Türk Dünyası Araştırmaları Vakfı, 1993), 35–36.

187 Gerber, *Position of Women in Ottoman Bursa, 1600–1700,* 233.

188 Jennings, *Women in Early 17th Century Ottoman Judicial Records/The Sharia Court of Anatolia Kayseri,* 67.

189 Fariba Zarinebaf-Shahr, "Women, Law and Imperial Justice in Ottoman Istanbul in the Late Seventeenth Century," in *Women, the Family, and Divorce Laws in Islamic History,* ed. Amira Al Azhary Sonbol. (Syracuse: Syracuse University Press, 1996), 90.

190 Gerber, *Position of Women in Ottoman Bursa, 1600–1700,* 233.

191 Jennings, *Women in Early 17th Century Ottoman Judicial Records,* 99.

192 Abraham Marcus, "Men, Women and Property: Dealers in Real Estate in 18th Century Aleppo," *Journal of the Economic and Social History of the Orient,* (May 26, 1983), 144.

193 Jennings, *Women in Early 17th Century Ottoman Judicial Records,* quoted from Ö. L. Barkan and Ekrem H. Ayverdi, *Istanbul Vakıfları Tahrir Defteri 935 (1546) Tarihli, Istanbul, 1970.*

194 Seng, 239.

195 Melman, 88.

196 Ibid., 144.

197 Ian C. Dengler, "Turkish Women in the Ottoman Empire: The Classical Age," *Women in the Muslim World*, ed. Lois Beck and Nikki Keddie, (Cambridge, Massachusetts–London, England: Harvard University Press, 1978), 235.

198 Cemal Kafadar, "The New Visibility of Sufism in Turkish Studies and Cultural Life," *The Dervish Lodge / Architecture, Art, and Sufism in Ottoman Turkey*, ed. Raymond Lifchez, (Berkeley, Los Angeles, Oxford: University of California Press), 308.

199 Sachiko Murata, *The Tao of Islam*, (Albany: State University of New York Press, 1992), 183.

200 Jalaluddin Rumi, *Discourses of RUMI*, trans. A. J. Arberry, (New York: Samuel Weiser, 1972), 92.

201 Idem, *Majalis-i sab'a*, 29 quoted in Murata, 62.

202 Bukhari, *Tawhid* 55; Muslim, *Tawba* 14.

203 "Then the Apostle goes on to give precedence to the feminine over the masculine, intending to convey thereby a special concern with and experience of women. Thus he says *thalath* [three] and not thalathah, which is used for numbering masculine nouns. This is remarkable, in that he also mentions perfume, which is a masculine noun, and the Arabs usually make the masculine gender prevail. Thus one would say, 'The Fatimas and Zaid went out [using the third person masculine plural],' and not the third person feminine plural. In this way they give preference to the masculine noun, even if there is only one such noun together with several feminine nouns. Now, although the Prophet was an Arab, he is here giving special attention to the significance of the love enjoined on him, seeing that he himself did not choose that love. It was God who taught him what he knew not, and God's bounty upon him was abundant. He therefore gave precedence to the feminine over the masculine by saying *thalath*. How knowledgeable was the Apostle concerning [spiritual] realities and how great was his concern for proper precedence.

"Furthermore, he made the final term [prayer] correspond to the first [women] in its femininity, placing the masculine term [perfume] between them. He begins with 'women' and ends with 'prayer,' both of which are feminine nouns, [the masculine noun] perfume coming in between them, as is the case with its existential being, since man is placed between the Essence [a feminine noun] from which he is manifested, and woman who is manifested from him. Thus he is between two feminine entities, the one substantially feminine, the other feminine in reality, women being feminine in reality, while prayer is not. Perfume is placed between them as Adam is situated between the Essence, which is the source of all existence, and Eve, whose existence stems from him.

"[Other terms] such as *sifah* [attribute] and *qudrah* {capability] are feminine. Indeed, whatever school of thought you adhere to, you will find feminine terms prominent. Even the Causalists say that God is the 'Cause' ['illah] of the Cosmos, and *'illa* is feminine." Ibn al-Arabi, *The Bezels of Wisdom*, trans. R.W.J. Austin, New Jersey, Paulist Press, 1980, pp. 277–278.

204 Ahnad ibn Hanbal I 191, 194 quoted from Murata, 215.

205 Jalaluddin Rumi, *Fihi ma fihi*, 176 quoted in Murata, 62.

206 Murata, 9, 69.

207 William Chittick, *The Sufi Path of Knowledge: Ibn al-Arabi's Metaphysics of Imagination*, (Albany, New York: Suny Press, 1989), 286.

Glossary of Turkish Words

bismillah	Prayer meaning "in the name of God"
çhibouk (çubuk)	Long pipe for smoking
denk	Bale
donum (dönüm)	About ¼ acre of land
ezan	Call to prayer
ferace	Cloak worn by Turkish women when they went out
hacı	Pilgrim to Mecca
hanım sultan	Daughter of the sultan's daughter
harem	Women's quarters / the sacred territory of Mecca and Medina
iftar	Meal that breaks fast during the holy month of Ramadan
imam	Prayer leader
kabul gün	Reception day for guests
kadın efendi	Title given to sultan's official concubine
kandil	One of four religious night celebrations with illimination of minarets
lohusa	Woman who has just given birth
mahalle	Neighborhood
müezzin	Caller to prayer
müftü	Muslim jurist
okka	Weight of 400 dirhems or 2.8 lbs.
selamlık	Quarters in Ottoman house reserved for males
sultan	Title given to head of Ottoman dynasty and his daughters
şehadet	Profession of faith
valide sultan	Queen mother
yaşmak	Veil worn by Ottoman women
yenge	Aunt or elderly woman who attends bride

Bibliography

Abdal-Rehim, Abdal-Rehim Abdal-Rahman. "The Family and Gender Laws in Egypt During the Ottoman Period." *Women, the Family and Divorce Laws in Islamic History*, pp. 96-111. ed. Amira Al Azhary Sonbol. Syracuse, New York: Syracuse University Press, 1996.

Akgündüz, Ahmet. *Osmanlı Kanunnâmeleri ve Hukukî Tahlilleri*. Vol. 7. Istanbul: Osmanlı Araştırmaları Vakfı Yayınları, 1994.

————*Osmanlı'da Harem*. Istanbul: Osmanlı Araştırmaları Vakfı Yayınları, 1995.

Amicus, Edmondo de. *Constantinople*. Paris: 1883.

Aydın, M. Akif. *Islam-Osmanlı Aile Hukuku*. Istanbul: Marmara Üniversitesi İlahiyat Fakültesi Yayınları No: 11, 1985.

Bates, Ülkü. "Women As Patrons of Architecture in Turkey." In *Women in the Muslim World*, pp. 245-260. ed. Lois Beck and Nikki Keddie. Cambridge, Massachusetts—London, England: Harvard University Press, 1978.

Bayraktar, Nimet. "Tarihte Hayırsever Türk Kadınları: Nurbanu Sultan – Kütüphanesi." *Kadın Gazetesi*, no. 541. (Jan. 15, 1959).

————"Tarihte Hayırsever Türk Kadınları: İsmihan Sultan ve Kütüphanesi." *Kadın Gazetesi*, no. 542. (Jan. 24, 1959).

————"Tarihte Hayırsever Türk Kadınları: Pertevniyal Sultan ve Kütüphanesi." *Kadın Gazetesi*, no. 549. (March 14, 1959).

————"Tarihte Hayırsever Türk Kadınları: Mihrimah Sultan ve Camiler." *Kadın Gazetesi*, no. 551. (March 28, 1959).

————"Tarihte Hayırsever Türk Kadınları: Mahpeker Sultan (Kösem Valide) ve Çinli Cami." *Kadın Gazetesi*, no. 533. (April 11, 1959).

————"Tarihte Hayırsever Türk Kadınları: Zeyneb Sultan ve Cami." *Kadın Gazetesi*, no. 559. (May 23, 1959).

Bezm-i Alem Valide Sultan Vakıf Gureba Hospital catalogue. Istanbul, 1987.

Blunt, Lady Fanny. *My Reminiscences*. London: John Murray, 1918/

Bukhari. *Al-Sahih*. "Kitab un-nikah."

Castellan, A. L. *Lettres Sur La Grecê, L'Hellespont et Constantinapole*. Vol. II. 1811.

Chittick, William. *The Sufi Path of Knowledge: Ibn al-Arabi's Metaphysics of Imagination*. Albany, New York: Suny Press. 1989.

Cooper, Elizabeth. *The Harem and The Purdah*. New Delhi: Bimla Publishing House, 1915.

Craven, Lady Elizabeth. *A Journey Through the Crimea to Constantinople in a Series of Letters Written in the Year 1786*. London: 1789.

Davis, Fanny. *The Ottoman Lady / A Social History from 1719 to 1918*. New York-Westport, Connecticut-London: Greenwood Press, 1986.

Dengler, Ian C. "Turkish Women in the Ottoman Empire: The Classical Age." In *Women in the Muslim World*, pp. 229-244. ed. Lois Beck and Nikki Keddie. Cambridge, Massachusetts – London, England: Harvard University Press, 1978.

Djevad, Ah. *Yabancilara Göre Eski Türkler*. Istanbul: Yağmur Yayınevi, 1974.

D'Ohsson, M. De M. *18. Yüzyıl Türkiye'sinde Örf ve Adetler*. tr. Zerhan Yüksel. Istanbul: Kervan Kitapçılık A.Ş.

Duben, Alan and Behar, Cem. *Istanbul Households / Marriage, Family and Fertility 1880-1940*. Cambridge: Cambridge University Press, 1991.

Esposito, John L. "Women's Rights In Islam." *Journal of Islamic Studies*. Vol. 14. pp. 99-114. (1975).

Ferriman, Z. Duckett. *Turkey and The Turks*. New York: The MacMillan Co., 1909.

Fontmagne, La Baronne Durand de. *Kırım Harbi Sonrasında Istanbul*. Istanbul: Kervan Kitapçılık Basın Sanayii ve Ticaret A. Ş., 1977.

Foundation for Establishing and Developing Historical Research and Documentation Centers. *Deeds of Trust of the Sultans Womenfolk*. Istanbul: 1990.

Garnett, Lucy M. J. *Home Life in Turkey*. New York: The MacMillan Co., 1909.

———*Turkey of the Ottomans*. London: 1911.

Gerber, Haim. "Social and Economic Position of Women in an Ottoman City, Bursa, 1600-1700." *International Journal of Middle East Studies*, 12. pp. 231-44. Cambridge: Cambridge University Press, 1980.

———*State, Society and Law in Islam—Ottoman Law in Comparative Perspective*. New York: State University of New York Press, 1994.

Inalcık, Halil. *The Ottoman Empire, The Classical Age 1300-1600*. London: Butler and Tanner Ltd., Frome and London, 1995.

Jennings, Ronald C. "Women in Early 17th Century Ottoman Judicial Records—Sharia Court of Anatolian Kayseri." *Journal of the Economic and Social History of the Orient* 18. pp. 53-114. (January 1975).

———*Christians and Muslims in Ottoman Cyprus and the Mediterranean World, 1571-1640*. New York and London: New York University Press, 1993.

Kafadar, Cemal. "The New Visibility of Sufism in Turkish Studies and Cultural Life." *The Dervish Lodge / Architecture, Art, and Sufism in Ottoman Turkey*. ed. Raymond Lifchez. Berkeley, Los Angeles, Oxford: University of California Press.

Krafft, H. U. *Türklerin Elinde Bir Alman Tacir- Ein Schwabischer Kaufmann in Türkischer Gefangenschaft*. tr. Turgut Akpınar. Istanbul: İletişim, 1996.

Kurt, Abdurrahman. *Tanzimat Döneminde Kadının Sosyo-Ekonomik Konumu, Bursa Örneği (1839-1836)*. Unpublished paper.

Kutay, Cemal. *Pembe Mendil*. Istanbul: Yeni Asya Yayınevi.

Mabro, Judy. *Veiled Half-Truths—Western Travelers' Perceptions of Middle Eastern Women*. London, New York: I. B. Tauris & Co Ltd. Publishers, 1991.

Marcus, Abraham. "Men, Women and Property: Dealers in Real Estate in Eighteenth Century Aleppo." *Journal of the Economic and Social History of the Orient* XXVI. 137-63. (May, 1983).

Melek Hanum. *Thirty Years in the Harem: or the Autobiography of Melek Hanum, Wife of H. H. Kıbrızlı Mehemmet Pasha*. London: Chapman and Hall, 1872.

Melman, Billie. *Women's Orients: English Women and the Middle East, 1718-1918 / Sexuality, Religion and Work*. London: MacMillan Academic and Professional Ltd., 1992.

Meriwether, Margaret. "The Rights of Children and the Responsibilities of Women—Women as Wasis in Ottoman Aleppo, 1770-1840." *Women, the Family, and Divorce Laws in Islamic History*. pp. 219-235. ed. Amira Al Azhary Sonbol. Syracuse, New York: Syracuse University Press, 1996.

Miller, Barnette. *Beyond The Sublime Porte / The Grand Seraglio of Stambul*. New Haven: Yale University Press, 1931.

Monroe, W. S. *Turkey and The Turks / An Account of the Lands, the Peoples and the Institutions of the Ottoman Empire*. New impression. London: Darf Publishers Limited, 1908 and 1985.

Montague, Lady Mary Wortley. *Letters from the Levant During the Embassy to Constantinople 1716-18*. Reprint. New York: Arno Press & The New York Times, 1971.

Murata, Sachiko. *The Tao of Islam / A Sourcebook on Gender Relationships in Islamic Thought*. Albany: State University of New York Press, 1992.

Murphy, Lynn. *Muslim Family Life in the Middle East as Depicted by Victorian Women Residents*. M. A. Thesis. McGill University, 1986.

Nahal, Galal el-. *The Judicial Administration of Ottoman Egypt in the Seventeenth Century*. Minneapolis: Bibliotheca Islamica, 1979.

Nasr, Seyyed Hossein. *An Introduction to Islamic Cosmological Doctrines*. Albany: State University of New York Press, 1993.

Ortaylı, İlber. *Osmanlı Toplumunda Aile*. Istanbul: Pan Yayıncılık, 2000.

Osmanoğlu, Ayşe. *Babam Sultan Abdülhamit / Hatıralarım*. 3rd ed. Ankara: Selçuk Yayınları, 1986.

Özdemir, Rifat. "Kırşehir'de Ailenin Sosyo-Ekonomik Yapısı: 1880-1906." *The Journal of Ottoman Studies* IX. pp. 101-57. (1989).

Öztürk, Said. "Osmanlı Ailesi Üzerine Düşünceler." *Ilim ve Sanat*. Vols. 44-45. Istanbul: Vefa Yayıncılık, 1997.

Pardoe, Julia. *City of the Sultan and Domestic Manners of the Turks in 1836*. 3 vols. 2nd ed. London: Henry Colburn, 1838.

Peirce, Leslie P. *The Imperial Harem / Women and Sovereignty in the Ottoman Empire*. New York – Oxford: Oxford University Press, 1993.

Penzer, N. M. *The Harem / An Account of the Institution As It Existed in the Palace of The Turkish Sultans With a History of the Grand Seraglio From its Foundation to the Present Time*. London – Bombay – Sydney: George G. Harrap & Co. Ltd., 1936.

Ramsey, W. M. *Every-Day Life in Turkey*. London: Hodder and Stoughton, 1897.

Rumi, Jallaluddin. *Discourses of Rumi*. trans. A. J. Arberry. New York: Samuel Weiser, 1972.

Said, Edward. *Orientalism*. New York: Pantheon Books, 1978.

Sancar, Aslı. *Osmanlı Toplumunda Kadın ve Aile*. Istanbul: Hanımlar Eğitim ve Kültür Vakfı Yayınları, 1999.

————"A Portrait of the Ottoman Woman." *Çerçeve*. pp. 115-119. January, 2000.

Saz, Leyla. *The Imperial Harem Of The Sultans / Memoirs of Leyla (Saz) Hanımefendi*. Istanbul: Peva Publications, 1994.

Seng, Yvonne J. "The Üsküdar Estates (Tereke) as Records of Everyday Life in an Ottoman Town, 1521-1524." Ph. D. dissertation. University of Chicago, 1991.

Seyfettin, Ömer. *Bahar ve Kelebek*. Istanbul: Inkılap ve AKA Basımevi, 1981.

Thevenot, Jean de. *1655-1656'da Istanbul ve Türkiye*. trans. Reşat Ekrem Koçu. Istanbul: Çığır Kitabevi, 1939.

Toledano, Ehud R. *Osmanlı Köle Ticareti 1840-1890*. trans. Y. Hakan Erdem. Istanbul: Tarih Vakfı Yurt Yayınları, 1994.

Tugay, Emine Fuat. *Three Centuries / Family Chronicles of Turkey and Egypt*. London: Oxford University Press, 1963.

Tuğlacı, Pars. *Women of Istanbul in Ottoman Times*. Vol. I. Istanbul: Altay Han Matbaası, 1984.

————*The Ottoman Palace Women*. Vol. III. Istanbul: Altay Han Matbaası, 1985.

Tulum, Mertol, ed. *Mühimme Defteri* 90. Istanbul: Türk Dünyasi AraştırmalarıVakfı, 1993.

Uluçay, Çağatay. *Harem*. 2nd ed. Ankara: Türk Tarih Kurumu Basımevi, 1985.

————*Padişahların Kadınları ve Kızları*. Ankara: Türk Tarih Kurumu Basımevi, 1980.

Uzunçarşılı, İsmail Hakkı. *Osmanlı Devletinin Saray Teşkilâtı*. 2nd ed. Ankara: Türk Tarih Kurumu Basımevi, 1984.

Walker, Mary Adelaid. *Eastern Life and Scenery, with Excursions in Asia Minor, Mytilene, Crete and Roumania*. London: Chapman and Hall, 1886.

Yusuf Ali, Abdullah. *The Holy Qur'an / Text, Translation and Commentary*. Washington DC: The American International Printing Company, 1946.

Zarinebaf-Shahr, Fariba. "Women, Law and Imperial Justice in the Eighteenth Century." *Women , the Family and Divorce Laws in Islamic History*. ed. Amira Al Azhary Sonbol. Syracuse, New York: Syracuse University Press, 1996.

————"Ottoman Women and the Tradition of Seeking Justice in the Eighteenth Century." *Women in the Ottoman Empire / Middle Eastern Women in the Early Modern Era*. pp. 253-263. ed. Madeline C. Zilfi. Leiden-New York-Köln: Brill, 1997.

Zilfi, Madeline C., ed. *Women in the Ottoman Empire / Middle Eastern Women in the Early Modern Era*. Leiden-New York- Köln: Brill, 1977.

Index